The Work of
the Afro-American Woman

THE SCHOMBURG LIBRARY OF
NINETEENTH-CENTURY BLACK WOMEN WRITERS

General Editor, Henry Louis Gates, Jr.

Titles are listed chronologically; collections that include works published over a span of years are listed according to the publication date of their initial work.

Phillis Wheatley, *The Collected Works of Phillis Wheatley*

Six Women's Slave Narratives: M. Prince; Old Elizabeth; M. J. Jackson; L. A. Delaney; K. Drumgoold; A. L. Burton

Spiritual Narratives: M. W. Stewart; J. Lee; J. A. J. Foote; V. W. Broughton

Ann Plato, *Essays*

Collected Black Women's Narratives: N. Prince; L. Picquet; B. Veney; S. K. Taylor

Frances E. W. Harper, *Complete Poems of Frances E. W. Harper*

Charlotte Forten Grimké, *The Journals of Charlotte Forten Grimké*

Mary Seacole, *Wonderful Adventures of Mrs. Seacole in Many Lands*

Harriet Jacobs, *Incidents in the Life of a Slave Girl*

Collected Black Women's Poetry, Volumes 1–4: M. E. Tucker; A. I. Menken; M. W. Fordham; P. J. Thompson; C. A. Thompson; H. C. Ray; L. A. J. Moorer; J. D. Heard; E. Bibb; M. P. Johnson; Mrs. H. Linden

Elizabeth Keckley, *Behind the Scenes. Or, Thirty Years a Slave, and Four Years in the White House*

C. W. Larison, M.D., *Silvia Dubois, A Biografy of the Slav Who Whipt Her Mistres and Gand Her Fredom*

Mrs. A. E. Johnson, *Clarence and Corinne; or, God's Way*

Octavia V. Rogers Albert, *The House of Bondage: or Charlotte Brooks and Other Slaves*

Emma Dunham Kelley, *Megda*

Anna Julia Cooper, *A Voice From the South*

Frances E. W. Harper, *Iola Leroy, or Shadows Uplifted*

Amanda Smith, *An Autobiography: The Story of the Lord's Dealings with Mrs. Amanda Smith the Colored Evangelist*

Mrs. A. E. Johnson, *The Hazeley Family*

Mrs. N. F. Mossell, *The Work of the Afro-American Woman*

Alice Dunbar-Nelson, *The Works of Alice Dunbar-Nelson*, Volumes 1–3

Emma D. Kelley-Hawkins, *Four Girls at Cottage City*

Pauline E. Hopkins, *Contending Forces: A Romance Illustrative of Negro Life North and South*

Pauline Hopkins, *The Magazine Novels of Pauline Hopkins*

Hallie Q. Brown, *Homespun Heroines and Other Women of Distinction*

The Work

of

the Afro-American Woman

MRS. N. F. MOSSELL

With an Introduction by
JOANNE BRAXTON

❧ ❧ ❧

❧ ❧ ❧

OXFORD UNIVERSITY PRESS

Oxford University Press

Oxford   New York   Toronto
Delhi   Bombay   Calcutta   Madras   Karachi
Petaling Jaya   Singapore   Hong Kong   Tokyo
Nairobi   Dar es Salaam   Cape Town
Melbourne   Auckland

and associated companies in
Berlin   Ibadan

First published in 1988 by Oxford University Press, Inc.,
200 Madison Avenue, New York, New York 10016

First issued as an Oxford University Press paperback, 1990

Oxford is a registered trademark of Oxford University Press

Library of Congress Cataloging-in-Publication Data

Mossell, N. F., Mrs. 1855–
The work of the Afro-American woman.
(The Schomburg library of nineteenth-century black
women writers)
Bibliography: p.
1. Afro-American women.   2. Afro-American women—
Poetry.   I. Title.   II. Series.
E185.86.M65   1988   305.8'96073   87-20353
ISBN 0-19-505265-X
ISBN 0-19-505267-6 (set)
ISBN 0-19-506326-0 (pbk.)

2 4 6 8 10 9 7 5 3 1

Printed in the United States of America

The
Schomburg Library
of
Nineteenth-Century
Black Women Writers
is
Dedicated
in Memory
of
Pauline Augusta Coleman Gates

1916–1987

PUBLISHER'S NOTE

FOREWORD
In Her Own Write

Henry Louis Gates, Jr.

One muffled strain in the Silent South, a jarring chord and a vague and uncomprehended cadenza has been and still is the Negro. And of that muffled chord, the one mute and voiceless note has been the sadly expectant Black Woman, ...

The "other side" has not been represented by one who "lives there." And not many can more sensibly realize and more accurately tell the weight and the fret of the "long dull pain" than the open-eyed but hitherto voiceless Black Woman of America.

. . . as our Caucasian barristers are not to blame if they cannot *quite* put themselves in the dark man's place, neither should the dark man be wholly expected fully and adequately to reproduce the exact Voice of the Black Woman.

—ANNA JULIA COOPER, *A Voice From the South* (1892)

The birth of the Afro-American literary tradition occurred in 1773, when Phillis Wheatley published a book of poetry. Despite the fact that her book garnered for her a remarkable amount of attention, Wheatley's journey to the printer had been a most arduous one. Sometime in 1772, a young African girl walked demurely into a room in Boston to undergo an oral examination, the results of which would determine the direction of her life and work. Perhaps she was shocked upon entering the appointed room. For there, perhaps gathered in a semicircle, sat eighteen of Boston's most notable citizens. Among them were John Erving, a prominent Boston merchant; the Reverend Charles Chauncy, pastor of the Tenth Congregational Church; and John Hancock, who would later gain fame for his signature on the Declaration of Independence. At the center of this group was His Excellency, Thomas Hutchinson, governor of Massachusetts, with Andrew Oliver, his lieutenant governor, close by his side.

Why had this august group been assembled? Why had it seen fit to summon this young African girl, scarcely eighteen years old, before it? This group of "the most respectable Characters in *Boston,*" as it would later define itself, had assembled to question closely the African adolescent on the slender sheaf of poems that she claimed to have "written by herself." We can only speculate on the nature of the questions posed to the fledgling poet. Perhaps they asked her to identify and explain—for all to hear—exactly who were the Greek and Latin gods and poets alluded to so frequently in her work. Perhaps they asked her to conjugate a verb in Latin or even to translate randomly selected passages from the Latin, which she and her master, John Wheatley, claimed that she "had made some Progress in." Or perhaps they asked her to recite from memory key passages from the texts of John Milton and Alexander Pope, the two poets by whom the African claimed to be most directly influenced. We do not know.

We do know, however, that the African poet's responses were more than sufficient to prompt the eighteen august gentlemen to compose, sign, and publish a two-paragraph "Attestation," an open letter "To the Publick" that prefaces Phillis Wheatley's book and that reads in part:

> We whose Names are under-written, do assure the World, that the Poems specified in the following Page, were (as we

verily believe) written by Phillis, a young Negro Girl, who
was but a few Years since, brought an uncultivated Barbarian
from *Africa*, and has ever since been, and now is, under the
Disadvantage of serving as a Slave in a Family in this Town.
She has been examined by some of the best Judges, and is
thought qualified to write them.

So important was this document in securing a publisher for
Wheatley's poems that it forms the signal element in the
prefatory matter preceding her *Poems on Various Subjects, Religious and Moral*, published in London in 1773.

Without the published "Attestation," Wheatley's publisher
claimed, few would believe that an African could possibly
have written poetry all by herself. As the eighteen put the
matter clearly in their letter, "Numbers would be ready to
suspect they were not really the Writings of Phillis." Wheatley and her master, John Wheatley, had attempted to publish
a similar volume in 1772 in Boston, but Boston publishers
had been incredulous. One year later, "Attestation" in hand,
Phillis Wheatley and her master's son, Nathaniel Wheatley,
sailed for England, where they completed arrangements for
the publication of a volume of her poems with the aid of the
Countess of Huntington and the Earl of Dartmouth.

This curious anecdote, surely one of the oddest oral examinations on record, is only a tiny part of a larger, and
even more curious, episode in the Enlightenment. Since the
beginning of the sixteenth century, Europeans had wondered aloud whether or not the African "species of men," as
they were most commonly called, *could* ever create formal
literature, could ever master "the arts and sciences." If they
could, the argument ran, then the African variety of humanity was fundamentally related to the European variety. If not,
then it seemed clear that the African was destined by nature

to be a slave. This was the burden shouldered by Phillis
Wheatley when she successfully defended herself and the authorship of her book against counterclaims and doubts.

Indeed, with her successful defense, Wheatley launched
two traditions at once—the black American literary tradition
and the black woman's literary tradition. If it is extraordinary
that not just one but both of these traditions were founded
simultaneously by a black woman—certainly an event unique
in the history of literature—it is also ironic that this important fact of common, coterminous literary origins seems to
have escaped most scholars.

That the progenitor of the black literary tradition was a
woman means, in the most strictly literal sense, that all subsequent black writers have evolved in a matrilinear line of
descent, and that each, consciously or unconsciously, has extended and revised a canon whose foundation was the poetry
of a black woman. Early black writers seem to have been
keenly aware of Wheatley's founding role, even if most of
her white reviewers were more concerned with the implications of her race than her gender. Jupiter Hammon, for example, whose 1760 broadside "An Evening Thought. Sal-
vation by Christ, With Penitential Cries" was the first
individual poem published by a black American, acknowl-
edged Wheatley's influence by selecting her as the subject of
his second broadside, "An Address to Miss Phillis Wheatly
[*sic*], Ethiopian Poetess, in Boston," which was published at
Hartford in 1778. And George Moses Horton, the second
Afro-American to publish a book of poetry in English (1829),
brought out in 1838 an edition of his *Poems By A Slave*
bound together with Wheatley's work. Indeed, for fifty-six
years, between 1773 and 1829, when Horton published *The
Hope of Liberty*, Wheatley was the *only* black person to have
published a book of imaginative literature in English. So

central was this black woman's role in the shaping of the
Afro-American literary tradition that, as one historian has
maintained, the history of the reception of Phillis Wheatley's
poetry *is* the history of Afro-American literary criticism. Well
into the nineteenth century, Wheatley and the black literary
tradition were the same entity.

But Wheatley is not the only black woman writer who
stands as a pioneering figure in Afro-American literature.
Just as Wheatley gave birth to the genre of black poetry, Ann
Plato was the first Afro-American to publish a book of essays
(1841) and Harriet E. Wilson was the first black person to
publish a novel in the United States (1859).

Despite this pioneering role of black women in the tradition, however, many of their contributions before this century have been all but lost or unrecognized. As Hortense
Spillers observed as recently as 1983,

> With the exception of a handful of autobiographical narratives
> from the nineteenth century, the black woman's realities are
> virtually suppressed until the period of the Harlem Renais-
> sance and later. Essentially the black woman as artist, as
> intellectual spokesperson for her own cultural apprenticeship,
> has not existed before, for anyone. At the source of [their]
> own symbol-making task, [the community of black women
> writers] confronts, therefore, a tradition of work that is quite
> recent, its continuities, broken and sporadic.

Until now, it has been extraordinarily difficult to establish
the formal connections between early black women's writing
and that of the present, precisely because our knowledge of
their work has been broken and sporadic. Phillis Wheatley,
for example, while certainly the most reprinted and discussed
poet in the tradition, is also one of the least understood. Ann
Plato's seminal work, *Essays* (which includes biographies and
poems), has not been reprinted since it was published a cen-

tury and a half ago. And Harriet Wilson's *Our Nig*, her compelling novel of a black woman's expanding consciousness in a racist Northern antebellum environment, never received even *one* review or comment at a time when virtually *all* works written by black people were heralded by abolitionists as salient arguments against the existence of human slavery. Many of the books reprinted in this set experienced a similar fate, the most dreadful fate for an author: that of being ignored then relegated to the obscurity of the rare book section of a university library. We can only wonder how many other texts in the black woman's tradition have been lost to this generation of readers or remain unclassified or uncatalogued and, hence, unread.

This was not always so, however. Black women writers dominated the final decade of the nineteenth century, perhaps spurred to publish by an 1886 essay entitled "The Coming American Novelist," which was published in *Lippincott's Monthly Magazine* and written by "A Lady From Philadelphia." This pseudonymous essay argued that the "Great American Novel" would be written by a black person. Her argument is so curious that it deserves to be repeated:

> When we come to formulate our demands of the Coming American Novelist, we will agree that he must be native-born. His ancestors may come from where they will, but we must give him a birthplace and have the raising of him. Still, the longer his family has been here the better he will represent us. Suppose he should have no country but ours, no traditions but those he has learned here, no longings apart from us, no future except in our future—the orphan of the world, he finds with us his home. And with all this, suppose he refuses to be fused into that grand conglomerate we call the "American type." With us, he is not of us. He is original, he has humor, he is tender, he is passive and fiery, he has been

taught what we call justice, and he has his own opinion about
it. He has suffered everything a poet, a dramatist, a novelist
need suffer before he comes to have his lips anointed. And
with it all he is in one sense a spectator, a little out of the
race. How would these conditions go towards forming an
original development? In a word, suppose the coming novelist
is of African origin? When one comes to consider the subject,
there is no improbability in it. One thing is certain,—our
great novel will not be written by the typical American.

An atypical American, indeed. Not only would the great
American novel be written by an African-American, it would
be written by an African-American *woman:*

> Yet farther: I have used the generic masculine pronoun
> because it is convenient; but Fate keeps revenge in store. It
> was a woman who, taking the wrongs of the African as her
> theme, wrote the novel that awakened the world to their
> reality, and why should not the coming novelist be a woman
> as well as an African? She—the woman of that race—has
> some claims on Fate which are not yet paid up.

It is these claims on fate that we seek to pay by publishing
The Schomburg Library of Nineteenth-Century Black Women
Writers.

This theme would be repeated by several black women
authors, most notably by Anna Julia Cooper, a prototypical
black feminist whose 1892 *A Voice From the South* can be
considered to be one of the original texts of the black feminist movement. It was Cooper who first analyzed the fallacy of referring to "the Black man" when speaking of black
people and who argued that just as white men cannot speak
through the consciousness of black men, neither can black
men "fully and adequately . . . reproduce the exact Voice of
the Black Woman." Gender and race, she argues, cannot be

conflated, except in the instance of a black woman's voice, and it is this voice which must be uttered and to which we must listen. As Cooper puts the matter so compellingly:

> It is not the intelligent woman vs. the ignorant woman; nor the white woman vs. the black, the brown, and the red,—it is not even the cause of woman vs. man. Nay, 'tis woman's strongest vindication for speaking that *the world needs to hear her voice*. It would be subversive of every human interest that the cry of one-half the human family be stifled. Woman in stepping from the pedestal of statue-like inactivity in the domestic shrine, and daring to think and move and speak,— to undertake to help shape, mold, and direct the thought of her age, is merely completing the circle of the world's vision. Hers is every interest that has lacked an interpreter and a defender. Her cause is linked with that of every agony that has been dumb—every wrong that needs a voice.
>
> It is no fault of man's that he has not been able to see truth from her standpoint. It does credit both to his head and heart that no greater mistakes have been committed or even wrongs perpetrated while she sat making tatting and snipping paper flowers. Man's own innate chivalry and the mutual interde- pendence of their interests have insured his treating her cause, in the main at least, as his own. And he is pardonably surprised and even a little chagrined, perhaps, to find his legislation not considered "perfectly lovely" in every respect. But in any case his work is only impoverished by her remaining dumb. The world has had to limp along with the wobbling gait and one-sided hesitancy of a man with one eye. Suddenly the bandage is removed from the other eye and the whole body is filled with light. It sees a circle where before it saw a segment. The darkened eye restored, every member rejoices with it.

The myopic sight of the darkened eye can only be restored when the full range of the black woman's voice, with its own special timbres and shadings, remains mute no longer.

Similarly, Victoria Earle Matthews, an author of short stories and essays, and a cofounder in 1896 of the National Association of Colored Women, wrote in her stunning essay, "The Value of Race Literature" (1895), that "when the literature of our race is developed, it will of necessity be different in all essential points of greatness, true heroism and real Christianity from what we may at the present time, for convenience, call American literature." Matthews argued that this great tradition of Afro-American literature would be the textual outlet "for the unnaturally suppressed inner lives which our people have been compelled to lead." Once these "unnaturally suppressed inner lives" of black people are unveiled, no "grander diffusion of mental light" will shine more brightly, she concludes, than that of the articulate Afro-American woman:

> And now comes the question, What part shall we women play in the Race Literature of the future? . . . within the compass of one small journal ["Woman's Era"] we have struck out a new line of departure—a journal, a record of Race interests gathered from all parts of the United States, carefully selected, moistened, winnowed and garnered by the ablest intellects of educated colored women, shrinking at no lofty theme, shirking no serious duty, aiming at every possible excellence, and determined to do their part in the future uplifting of the race.
>
> If twenty women, by their concentrated efforts in one literary movement, can meet with such success as has engendered, planned out, and so successfully consummated this convention, what much more glorious results, what wider spread success, what grander diffusion of mental light will not come forth at the bidding of the enlarged hosts of women writers, already called into being by the stimulus of your efforts?
>
> And here let me speak one word for my journalistic sisters

who have already entered the broad arena of journalism. Before the "Woman's Era" had come into existence, no one except themselves can appreciate the bitter experience and sore disappointments under which they have at all times been compelled to pursue their chosen vocations.

If their brothers of the press have had their difficulties to contend with, I am here as a sister journalist to state, from the fullness of knowledge, that their task has been an easy one compared with that of the colored woman in journalism.

Woman's part in Race Literature, as in Race building, is the most important part and has been so in all ages. . . . All through the most remote epochs she has done her share in literature. . . .

One of the most important aspects of this set is the republication of the salient texts from 1890 to 1910, which literary historians could well call "The Black Woman's Era." In addition to Mary Helen Washington's definitive edition of Cooper's *A Voice From the South*, we have reprinted two novels by Amelia Johnson, Frances Harper's *Iola Leroy*, two novels by Emma Dunham Kelley, Alice Dunbar-Nelson's two impressive collections of short stories, and Pauline Hopkins's three serialized novels as well as her monumental novel, *Contending Forces*—all published between 1890 and 1910. Indeed, black women published more works of fiction in these two decades than black men had published in the previous half century. Nevertheless, this great achievement has been ignored.

Moreover, the writings of nineteenth-century Afro-American women in general have remained buried in obscurity, accessible only in research libraries or in overpriced and poorly edited reprints. Many of these books have never been reprinted at all; in some instances only one or two copies are extant. In these works of fiction, poetry, autobiography, biography, essays, and journalism resides the mind of the nineteenth-century Afro-American woman. Until these works are made readily available to teachers and their students, a significant segment of the black tradition will remain silent.

Oxford University Press, in collaboration with the Schomburg Center for Research in Black Culture, is publishing thirty volumes of these compelling works, each of which contains an introduction by an expert in the field. The set includes such rare texts as Johnson's *The Hazeley Family* and *Clarence and Corinne,* Plato's *Essays,* the most complete edition of Phillis Wheatley's poems and letters, Emma Dunham Kelley's pioneering novel *Megda,* several previously unpublished stories and a novel by Alice Dunbar-Nelson, and the first collected volumes of Pauline Hopkins's three serialized novels and Frances Harper's poetry. We also present four volumes of poetry by such women as Mary Eliza Tucker Lambert, Adah Menken, Josephine Heard, and Maggie Johnson. Numerous slave and spiritual narratives, a newly discovered novel—*Four Girls at Cottage City*—by Emma Dunham Kelley (-Hawkins), and the first American edition of *Wonderful Adventures of Mrs. Seacole in Many Lands* are also among the texts included.

In addition to resurrecting the works of black women authors, it is our hope that this set will facilitate the resurrection of the Afro-American woman's literary tradition itself by unearthing its nineteenth-century roots. In the works of Nella Larsen and Jessie Fauset, Zora Neale Hurston and Ann Petry, Lorraine Hansberry and Gwendolyn Brooks, Paule Marshall and Toni Cade Bambara, Audre Lorde and Rita Dove, Toni Morrison and Alice Walker, Gloria Naylor and Jamaica Kincaid, these roots have branched luxuriantly. The eighteenth- and nineteenth-century authors whose works are presented in this set founded and nurtured the black women's literary tradition, which must be revived, explicated, analyzed, and debated before we can understand more completely the formal shaping of this tradition within a tradition, a coded literary universe through which, regrettably, we are only just beginning to navigate our way. As Anna Cooper said nearly one hundred years ago, we have been blinded by the loss of sight in one eye and have therefore been unable to detect the full *shape* of the Afro-American literary tradition.

Literary works configure into a tradition not because of some mystical collective unconscious determined by the biology of race or gender, but because writers read other writers and *ground* their representations of experience in models of language provided largely by other writers to whom they feel akin. It is through this mode of literary revision, amply evident in the *texts* themselves—in formal echoes, recast metaphors, even in parody—that a "tradition" emerges and defines itself.

This is formal bonding, and it is only through formal bonding that we can know a literary tradition. The collective publication of these works by black women now, for the first time, makes it possible for scholars and critics, male and female, black and white, to *demonstrate* that black women writers read, and revised, other black women writers. To demonstrate this set of formal literary relations is to demonstrate that sexuality, race, and gender are both the condition and the basis of *tradition*—but tradition as found in discrete acts of language use.

A word is in order about the history of this set. For the past decade, I have taught a course, first at Yale and then at Cornell, entitled "Black Women and Their Fictions," a course that I inherited from Toni Morrison, who developed it in

the mid-1970s for Yale's Program in Afro-American Studies. Although the course was inspired by the remarkable accomplishments of black women novelists since 1970, I gradually extended its beginning date to the late nineteenth century,
studying Frances Harper's *Iola Leroy* and Anna Julia Cooper's *A Voice From the South*, both published in 1892. With
the discovery of Harriet E. Wilson's seminal novel, *Our Nig*
(1859), and Jean Yellin's authentication of Harriet Jacobs's
brilliant slave narrative, *Incidents in the Life of a Slave Girl*
(1861), a survey course spanning over a century and a quarter
emerged.

But the discovery of *Our Nig*, as well as the interest in
nineteenth-century black women's writing that this discovery
generated, convinced me that even the most curious and
diligent scholars knew very little of the extensive history
of the creative writings of Afro-American women before
1900. Indeed, most scholars of Afro-American literature
had never even read most of the books published by black
women, simply because these books—of poetry, novels, short
stories, essays, and autobiography—were mostly accessible only
in rare book sections of university libraries. For reasons un-
clear to me even today, few of these marvelous renderings of
the Afro-American woman's consciousness were reprinted in
the late 1960s and early 1970s, when so many other texts of
the Afro-American literary tradition were resurrected from
the dark and silent graveyard of the out-of-print and were
reissued in facsimile editions aimed at the hungry readership
for canonical texts in the nascent field of black studies.

So, with the help of several superb research assistants—
including David Curtis, Nicola Shilliam, Wendy Jones, Sam
Otter, Janadas Devan, Suvir Kaul, Cynthia Bond, Elizabeth
Alexander, and Adele Alexander—and with the expert advice

of scholars such as William Robinson, William Andrews, Mary Helen Washington, Maryemma Graham, Jean Yellin, Houston A. Baker, Jr., Richard Yarborough, Hazel Carby, Joan R. Sherman, Frances Foster, and William French, dozens of bibliographies were used to compile a list of books written or narrated by black women mostly before 1910. Without the assistance provided through this shared experience of scholarship, the scholar's true legacy, this project could not have been conceived. As the list grew, I was struck by how very many of these titles that I, for example, had never even heard of, let alone read, such as Ann Plato's *Essays*, Louisa Picquet's slave narrative, or Amelia Johnson's two novels, *Clarence and Corinne* and *The Hazeley Family*. Through our research with the Black Periodical Fiction and Poetry Project (funded by NEH and the Ford Foundation), I also realized that several novels by black women, including three works of fiction by Pauline Hopkins, had been serialized in black periodicals, but had never been collected and published as books. Nor had the several books of poetry published by black women, such as the prolific Frances E. W. Harper, been collected and edited. When I discovered still another "lost" novel by an Afro-American woman (*Four Girls at Cottage City*, published in 1898 by Emma Dunham Kelley-Hawkins), I decided to attempt to edit a collection of reprints of these works and to publish them as a "library" of black women's writings, in part so that I could read them myself.

Convincing university and trade publishers to undertake this project proved to be a difficult task. Despite the commercial success of *Our Nig* and of the several reprint series of women's works (such as Virago, the Beacon Black Women Writers Series, and Rutgers' American Women Writers Series), several presses rejected the project as "too large," "too limited," or as "commercially unviable." Only two publishers recognized the viability and the import of the project and, of these, Oxford's commitment to publish the titles simultaneously as a set made the press's offer irresistible.

While attempting to locate original copies of these exceedingly rare books, I discovered that most of the texts were housed at the Schomburg Center for Research in Black Culture, a branch of The New York Public Library, under the direction of Howard Dodson. Dodson's infectious enthusiasm for the project and his generous collaboration, as well as that of his stellar staff (especially Diana Lachatanere, Sharon Howard, Ellis Haizip, Richard Newman, and Betty Gubert), led to a joint publishing initiative that produced this set as part of the Schomburg's major fund-raising campaign. Without Dodson's foresight and generosity of spirit, the set would not have materialized. Without William P. Sisler's masterful editorship at Oxford and his staff's careful attention to detail, the set would have remained just another grand idea that tends to languish in a scholar's file cabinet.

I would also like to thank Dr. Michael Winston and Dr. Thomas C. Battle, Vice-President of Academic Affairs and the Director of the Moorland-Spingarn Research Center (respectively) at Howard University, for their unending encouragement, support, and collaboration in this project, and Esme E. Bhan at Howard for her meticulous research and bibliographical skills. In addition, I would like to acknowledge the aid of the staff at the libraries of Duke University, Cornell University (especially Tom Weissinger and Donald Eddy), the Boston Public Library, the Western Reserve Historical Society, the Library of Congress, and Yale University. Linda Robbins, Marion Osmun, Sarah Flanagan, and Gerard Case, all members of the staff at Oxford, were extraordinarily effective at coordinating, editing, and producing the various segments of each text in the set. Candy Ruck, Nina de Tar, and Phillis Molock expertly typed reams of correspondence and manuscripts connected to the project.

I would also like to express my gratitude to my colleagues who edited and introduced the individual titles in the set. Without their attention to detail, their willingness to meet strict deadlines, and their sheer enthusiasm for this project, the set could not have been published. But finally and ultimately, I would hope that the publication of the set would help to generate even more scholarly interest in the black women authors whose work is presented here. Struggling against the seemingly insurmountable barriers of racism *and* sexism, while often raising families and fulfilling full-time professional obligations, these women managed nevertheless to record their thoughts and feelings and to *testify* to all who dare read them that the will to harness the power of collective endurance and survival is the will to write.

The Schomburg Library of Nineteenth-Century Black Women Writers is dedicated in memory of Pauline Augusta Coleman Gates, who died in the spring of 1987. It was she who inspired in me the love of learning and the love of literature. I have encountered in the books of this set no will more determined, no courage more noble, no mind more sublime, no self more celebratory of the achievements of all Afro-American women, and indeed of life itself, than her own.

A NOTE FROM
THE SCHOMBURG CENTER

Howard Dodson

The Schomburg Center for Research in Black Culture, The New York Public Library, is pleased to join with Dr. Henry Louis Gates and Oxford University Press in presenting The Schomburg Library of Nineteenth-Century Black Women Writers. This thirty-volume set includes the work of a generation of black women whose writing has only been available previously in rare book collections. The materials reprinted in twenty-four of the thirty volumes are drawn from the unique holdings of the Schomburg Center.

A research unit of The New York Public Library, the Schomburg Center has been in the forefront of those institutions dedicated to collecting, preserving, and providing access to the records of the black past. In the course of its two generations of acquisition and conservation activity, the Center has amassed collections totaling more than 5 million items. They include over 100,000 bound volumes, 85,000 reels and sets of microforms, 300 manuscript collections containing some 3.5 million items, 300,000 photographs and extensive holdings of prints, sound recordings, film and videotape, newspapers, artworks, artifacts, and other book and nonbook materials. Together they vividly document the history and cultural heritages of people of African descent worldwide.

Though established some sixty-two years ago, the Center's book collections date from the sixteenth century. Its oldest item, an Ethiopian Coptic Tunic, dates from the eighth or ninth century. Rare materials, however, are most available for the nineteenth-century African-American experience. It is from these holdings that the majority of the titles selected for inclusion in this set are drawn.

The nineteenth century was a formative period in African-American literary and cultural history. Prior to the Civil War, the majority of black Americans living in the United States were held in bondage. Law and practice forbade teaching them to read or write. Even after the war, many of the impediments to learning and literary productivity remained. Nevertheless, black men and women of the nineteenth century persevered in both areas. Moreover, more African-Americans than we yet realize turned their observations, feelings, social viewpoints, and creative impulses into published works. In time, this nineteenth-century printed record included poetry, short stories, histories, novels, autobiographies, social criticism, and theology, as well as economic and philosophical treatises. Unfortunately, much of this body of literature remained, until very recently, relatively inaccessible to twentieth-century scholars, teachers, creative artists, and others interested in black life. Prior to the late 1960s, most Americans (black as well as white) had never heard of these nineteenth-century authors, much less read their works.

The civil rights and black power movements created unprecedented interest in the thought, behavior, and achievements of black people. Publishers responded by revising traditional texts, introducing the American public to a new generation of African-American writers, publishing a variety of thematic anthologies, and reprinting a plethora of "classic texts" in African-American history, literature, and art. The reprints usually appeared as individual titles or in a series of bound volumes or microform formats.

The Schomburg Center, which has a long history of supporting publishing that deals with the history and culture of Africans in diaspora, became an active participant in many of the reprint revivals of the 1960s. Since hard copies of original printed works are the preferred formats for producing facsimile reproductions, publishers frequently turned to the Schomburg Center for copies of these original titles. In addition to providing such material, Schomburg Center staff members offered advice and consultation, wrote introductions, and occasionally entered into formal copublishing arrangements in some projects.

Most of the nineteenth-century titles reprinted during the 1960s, however, were by and about black men. A few black women were included in the longer series, but works by lesser known black women were generally overlooked. The Schomburg Library of Nineteenth-Century Black Women Writers is both a corrective to these previous omissions and an important contribution to Afro-American literary history in its own right. Through this collection of volumes, the thoughts, perspectives, and creative abilities of nineteenth-century African-American women, as captured in books and pamphlets published in large part before 1910, are again being made available to the general public. The Schomburg Center is pleased to be a part of this historic endeavor.

I would like to thank Professor Gates for initiating this project. Thanks are due both to him and Mr. William P. Sisler of Oxford University Press for giving the Schomburg Center an opportunity to play such a prominent role in the set. Thanks are also due to my colleagues at The New York Public Library and the Schomburg Center, especially Dr. Vartan Gregorian, Richard De Gennaro, Paul Fasana, Betsy

Pinover, Richard Newman, Diana Lachatanere, Glenderlyn Johnson, and Harold Anderson for their assistance and support. I can think of no better way of demonstrating than in this set the role the Schomburg Center plays in assuring that the black heritage will be available for future generations.

INTRODUCTION

Joanne Braxton

In the introduction to her *When and Where I Enter: The Impact of Black Women on Race and Sex in America* (1984), cultural historian Paula Giddings posits:

> In the racial struggle—in slavery and freedom—they fought every way that men did. In the feminist battle they demanded the same protection and properties that the "best" White women enjoyed, but at the same time redefined the meaning of what was called "true womanhood." For the Black woman argued that her experience under slavery, her participation in the work force, and her sense of independence made her more of a woman, not less of one. (p. 7)

Mrs. N. F. Mossell's *The Work of the Afro-American Woman* (1894) represents an early attempt to articulate this black and feminist viewpoint, which takes race, not sex, as its point of departure. *The Work* presented black women and their accomplishments to a wider sphere of humanity and redefined "true womanhood" by challenging its "cardinal tenets" with race-centered analysis. In addition to "defending the name" of the black woman against her detractors, *The Work* offered her a source of instruction and inspiration. Today, *The Work* remains a valuable document of black American cultural and intellectual history, as well as a link between the past and the present. It was, for the black woman of the 1890s, the equivalent of Giddings' work of the 1980s—in sum, a powerful and progressive statement.

The author, Mrs. Gertrude E. H. Bustill Mossell (1855–1948), wrote under the initials of her husband, Dr. Nathan

Francis Mossell (1856–1946), a graduate of the University of Pennsylvania Medical School and founder of the Frederick Douglass Memorial Hospital in Philadelphia. By this strategy of public modesty, the author signaled her intention to defend and celebrate black womanhood without disrupting the delicate balance of black male-female relations or challenging masculine authority. She would be a "race woman" first; she would promote the cause of her sisters, and she would do so in a context that would elevate the entire race. Thus she invited and received the enthusiastic support of influential black men and spread her mission further than if she had taken a different track.

The daughter of black Quakers who later became Presbyterians, Gertrude E. H. Bustill descended from a family "whose wealth and activism could be traced to the eighteenth century" (Giddings, p. 30). She received an excellent education in the public schools of Philadelphia and later taught in the public-school systems in Philadelphia, Camden, New Jersey, and Frankfort, Kentucky. As a journalist she wrote for various publications, including the *Philadelphia Press, Times,* and *Inquirer,* the *Indianapolis Freeman,* the *Richmond Rankin Institute,* and *Our Women and Children.* After her marriage to Dr. Mossell in 1893 and the subsequent birth of two daughters, she continued her career with syndicated columns and articles in *The Philadelphia Echo, The Philadelphia Times, The Independent,* and the *Press Republican.* Additionally, she edited the "Woman's Department" of the *New York Age, the Indianapolis World,* and the *New York Freeman.* She also contributed to the *A.M.E. Church Review. The Work of the Afro-American Woman* was one of Mrs. Mossell's two books; the other was *Little Dansie's One Day at Sabbath School* (1902), a children's book.

The Work of the Afro-American Woman brings together intellectual goals and black feminist politics in the spirit of racial uplift. A collection of original essays and poems, this eclectic volume is part intellectual history, part advice book, and part polemic. As a celebration of the achievements of Afro-American women, this volume is inherently feminist; as a public and sometimes political statement, it is, in many ways, a radical product for its time.

Mrs. Mossell's work is made palatable to her audience by her public modesty and strict adherence to a code of race-conscious womanhood and black Christian motherhood. The prototypical black feminist, she speaks as a mother and dedicates *The Work of the Afro-American Woman* to her daughters, "praying they may grow into a pure and noble womanhood." In her preface, she presents *The Work* as a "note of inspiration . . . for the budding womanhood of the race." Her stated goal, therefore, is the development of "womanhood," specifically black womanhood.

In his introduction to *The Work*, AME Bishop Benjamin F. Lee authenticated Mrs. Mossell's "educative cause." "When the women of any race become intelligent and active in literary pursuits," the bishop wrote, "that race has acquired the greatest guarantee of success." "This book will not only have that influence upon the world which comes from the consideration mentioned above," he added, "but, being thoughtfully prepared with a view to impressing a growing race with the importance of a correct life and independent thought, it must add largely to the educative cause of that race" (p. 3). In comparing the relationship of the author and "a growing race" with that of a mother and child, the bishop's statement sustains mutually the maternal virtues of ideal womanhood and the political goals of racial uplift. This affirmation by a ranking member of the hierarchy of the most powerful middle-class black religious denomination serves as a seal of masculine approval. In this volume, the bishop hereby attests, Mrs. Mossell has done her duty as a woman, a Christian, and a mother.

The Work itself is divided into two sections, the first a series of essays and the second a collection of poems. The essays treat topics related to the development of the literature and culture of black American women. In addition to the title piece, "The Work of the Afro-American Woman," essays include "A Sketch of Afro-American Literature," "The Afro-American Woman in Verse," "Our Women in Journalism," "Our Afro-American Representatives at the World's Fair," "The Opposite Point of View," "A Lofty Study," and "Caste in Institutions."

Mrs. Mossell celebrates the accomplishments of her sex and her race as the result of communal and cooperative efforts; her analysis looks back to the tradition of Harriet Tubman and Sojourner Truth, and at the same time it treats the diverse achievements of contemporaries and peers as sources of inspiration as it looks toward the future. The title essay, "The Work of the Afro-American Woman," links black emancipation from enslavement with the cause of women's rights. In Mrs. Mossell's analysis:

> The emancipation of the Negro race came about at the entrance to that which has been aptly termed the Woman's Century; co-education, higher education for women, had each gained a foothold. The "Woman's Suffrage" movement had passed the era of ridicule and entered upon that of critical study. The Woman's Christian Temperance Union had become a strong factor in the reform work of the nation. These facts made the uplifting of the womanhood of this race a more

hopeful task than might otherwise have been, and gave to the individual woman of the race opportunities to reach a higher plane of development with less effort than would have been possible under a more unfavorable aspect of the woman question. Trammelled by their past condition and its consequent poverty, combined with the blasting influence of caste prejudice, they have yet made a fair showing. (pp. 9–10)

"The Work of the Afro-American Woman" chronicles the achievements of educators, writers, journalists, dramatists, composers, missionaries, and businesswomen. The large number of distinguished educators includes such familiar names as Fanny Coppin, Edwina Kruse, Anna Julia Cooper, Lucy Moten, Lucy Laney, and others, graduates of Oberlin, Fisk, Howard, Scotia, Shaw, Tuskegee, Livingstone, and New York University, all of them women engaged in the uplift of the race. Included among the numerous writers and journalists are Phillis Wheatley, F. E. W. Harper, Anna Julia Cooper, Josephine Heard, Amanda Smith, Ida B. Wells, Lucinda Bragg, Josephine Ruffin, Alice Ruth Moore (later Dunbar-Nelson), and Mrs. I. Garland Penn. Among the businesswomen that Mrs. Mossell includes are undertakers, farmers, prospectors, inventors, hotel and innkeepers, and women in the ice trade and the sand-hauling business.

She even discovered a Revolutionary War soldier! Of particular interest is "Deborah Gannet, who had enlisted during the Revolutionary war in Captain Wells' company, under the name of Robert Shurtliffe, serving from May, 1782, until October 23, 1783." According to the author, Gannet "discharged the duties of her office and at the same time, preserved inviolate the virtue of her sex, and was granted therefore a pension of thirty-four pounds" (p. 26). She goes on to catalogue doctors, lawyers, and missionaries, all by name and institutional affiliation.

In praising missionaries and others celebrated for their sacrifice, courage, and perseverence, Mrs. Mossell notes, "[M]any of our women have turned aside from laboring for their individual success and given thought to the condition of the weak and suffering classes" (p. 28). Among these women are Harriet Tubman, Sojourner Truth, Ida B. Wells, and the early organizers of mission schools and homes, orphanages and benevolent associations. Mrs. Mossell also pays tribute to the plantation wife, whom she calls "the most humble of our women" (p. 23). Struggling against Jim Crow, poverty, and what Mrs. Mossell politely calls "caste prejudice," these women elevated themselves and "raised a race." In short, Mrs. Mossell argues, "The women of this race have always been industrious, however much the traducers of the race may attempt to make it appear otherwise" (p. 22).

In the conclusion to her title essay, Mrs. Mossell softens her stance and ends with a flourish that is also an appeal to her white and female readers: "Will not our more favored sisters, convinced of our desires and aspirations because of these first few feeble efforts, stretch out the helping hand that we may rise to a nobler, purer womanhood?" (p. 47). The significance of this plea becomes more evident against the backdrop of industrialization and the Victorian values of the so-called "cult of true womanhood." According to Paula Giddings, Northern industrialization created among white women "a new middle class striving for upper class status" and a "cult of the lady" that served as "the vehicle for these aspirations" (p. 47). "The true woman's exclusive role was as homemaker, mother, housewife and family tutor of the social and moral graces," Giddings adds (p. 47). "Since only women of leisure could even hope to join the pantheon of ladyhood, true women, with all the attendant moral implications, became virtually synonymous with the upper class" (Giddings, p. 48). Excluded from the industrialized labor force as well as from the protections of a Victorian code of morality, black women rebelled against the racist and classist assumptions of "the cult of the lady" and aspired instead to a "noble womanhood" that would be meaningful in the context of their day-to-day experience. *The Work* presents black women's exemplary achievements to their white sisters as evidence that black women were capable of rising to "a nobler, purer womanhood," if white women would "stretch out the helping hand" of sisterly aid and protection. The inclusive vision of "nobler, purer womanhood" that these black women strived for applied to working-class women as well as to professionals and homemakers. Moreover, it substituted the value of race-conscious activism for the submissiveness of the lady. Therefore, much is implied in Mrs. Mossell's closing flourish. *The Work* itself becomes a metaphor for the struggle of American women of color to attain a dignified and self-conscious womanhood and to raise themselves (and the race itself) in the regard of the dominant culture.

In "A Sketch of Afro-American Literature," Mrs. Mossell comments about the cultural value of intellectual history to the people who invent it. "The intellectual history of a people or nation constitutes to a great degree the heart of its life." Of the literary strivings of "native Africans made Americans against their will," she writes: "With all its drawbacks the race has built up a literature of its own that must be studied by the future historian of the life of the American nation." She then adds that "Afro-Americans are born idealists; in them art, poetry, music, oratory, all lie sleeping" (pp. 48–51, 55). In 1894, less than thirty years after the amendment of the Constitution to prohibit black enslavement and more than forty-five years before women received the vote, Mrs. Mossell defined and documented a tradition of black women writers. In "The Afro-American Woman in Verse," she celebrates such "sweet singers" as Phillis Wheatley, Sarah Forten, Frances E. W. Harper, Charlotte Forten Grimké, Cordelia Ray, Mary Ashe Lee, Alice Ruth Moore, and others. She quotes Mary Ashe Lee's stunning "Afmerica":

> Hang up the harp! I hear them say,
> Nor sing again an Afric lay,
> The time has passed; we would forget—
> And sadly now do we regret
> There still remains a single trace
> Of that dark shadow of disgrace,
> Which tarnished long a race's fame
> Until she blushed at her own name;
> And now she stands unbound and free,
> In that full sight of liberty.
> "Sing not her past!" cries out a host,
> "Nor of her future stand and boast.
> Oblivion be her aimed-for goal,
> In which to cleanse her ethnic soul,
> And coming out a creature new,
> On life's arena stand in view."
> But stand with no identity?
> All robbed of personality?
> Perhaps, this is the nobler way
> To teach that wished-for brighter day.
> Yet shall the good which she has done
> Be silenced all and never sung?
> And shall she have no inspirations
> To elevate her expectations?   (p. 84)

In this feminized "Afmerica," the race becomes woman and the woman becomes a race overflowing with both inspirations and expectations. Mrs. Mossell incorporates not fewer than twenty complete poems by black women poets, many of them her contemporaries, in this polemical plea for the recognition of the poetic talents of her sisters and the traditions from which they descended.

Perhaps the most polemical of all the essays in *The Work* is "The Opposite Point of View," a "womanist" argument for greater equality in marital relationships. This essay undercuts stereotypes traditionally associated with the nineteenth-century cult of true womanhood and redefines them in a black and feminist context.

Mrs. Mossell's expressed interest is that of the black woman, which is presumed to be "opposite" the masculine point of view on sexuality, courtship, marriage, and home and family life. This alternative viewpoint is epitomized by the wry quip of one "refined feminine observer": " 'Honey, courting is mighty pretty business; but courting is no more like marrying than chalk is like cheese' " (p. 117). "The Opposite Point of View" challenges turn-of-the-century conventions of "women's place" in male-female relations and in home and family life. "I may not be orthodox," Mrs. Mosell writes,

> but I venture to assert that keeping a clean house will not keep a man at home; to be sure it will not drive him out, but neither will it keep him in to a very large extent. And you, dear tender-hearted darlings, that are being taught daily that it will, might as well know the truth now and not be crying your eyes out later.

She goes on to advocate and explicate her viewpoint:

> Women must not be blamed because they are not equal to the self-sacrifice of always meeting husbands with a smile, nor

the wife blamed that she does not dress after marriage as she dressed before; child-birth and nursing, the care of the sick through sleepless, nightly vigils, the exactions and irritations incident to a life whose duties are made up of trifles and interruptions, and whose work of head and heart never ceases, make it an impossibility to put behind them at all times all cares and smile with burdened heart and weary feet and brain. (pp. 119–21)

Balancing this somewhat acerbic view of marriage, Mrs. Mossell becomes the advocate of "the good husband." "A good husband will do his duty even if the wife fails, as so many wives are doing to-day with bad husbands," she asserts (p. 122).

"The Opposite Point of View" concludes with Mrs. Mossell's prescription for a happy home life:

The home should be founded on right principles, on morality, Christian living, a due regard to heredity and environment that promise good for the future. With these taken into consideration, backed by love, or even true regard, each having an abiding sense of duty and a desire to carry out its principles, no marriage so contracted can ever prove a failure. (p. 125)

Beneath the elaborate rhetoric, the author calls for a new definition of the relationship between men and women and a new equality in marriage based on "true regard" and mutual understanding. The author's advice-essay formula and genteel Christian rhetoric soften the barb of her criticism somewhat, yet "The Opposite Point of View" was a radical statement on family life and marital relations in a time when their success was seen primarily as the woman's responsibility. Taken as a whole, this essay stands as a valuable document of the sexual politics of black America.

Mrs. Mossell's ideas of simplicity, economy, and mutuality are decidedly influenced by her Quaker background and her admiration for Quaker values. These values extend beyond her view of male-female relations to the act of writing itself. "A Lofty Study" describes her visit to the attic library of a member of the Society of Friends: "Neatness, order, comfort reigned supreme. Not a sound from the busy street reached us. It was so quiet, so peaceful, the air was so fresh and pure, it seemed like living in a new atmosphere." Inspired by this visit, Mrs. Mossell recommends, on general principle, the "unused attic" as the "very room for a study" (p. 127). She was years ahead of Virginia Woolf in advocating the writer's need for "a room of one's own." In her words, such a study offers "a place to one's self without disturbing the household economy" (p. 128).

Benefits will accrue to the woman who designs her own "lofty study," Mrs. Mossell asserts.

> Even when there is a library in the home, it is used by the whole family, and if the husband is literary in his tastes, he often desires to occupy it exclusively at the very time you have leisure, perhaps. Men are so often educated to work alone that even sympathetic companionship annoys. Very selfish, we say, but we often find it so—and therefore the necessity of a study of one's own. (p. 128)

The use of the detached editorial "we" puts some distance between the audience and the force of the commentary, including the implied criticism of masculine selfishness and the way that men are educated.

Mrs. Mossell strengthens her subversive rhetorical strategy by returning to the advice formula at the conclusion of the essay:

What a satisfaction to put everything in order, turn the key, and feel that all is safe—no busy hands, no stray breeze can carry away or disarrange some choice idea kept for the future delectation by the public! Besides this, one who writes much generally finds that she can write best at some certain spot. Ideas come more rapidly, sentences take more lucid forms. Very often the least change from that position will break up the train of thought. (p. 129)

This sketch is an object lesson for women writers seeking the privacy and consecutive work hours necessary to write amidst their individual cares and responsibilities. It suggests the creation of a private work space as a means of bringing about a desired end—the written "work." Despite the romantic view of the writer's garret and the subdued tone of the essay itself, Mrs. Mossell's message and her sexual politics remain clear.

Mrs. Mossell's racial politics are perhaps most evident in the final essay, "Caste in Institutions." This essay attacks the reluctance of (white-controlled) "institutions devoted exclusively to Negro education" to employ "colored men" on their faculties:

The *continued failure* of these institutions to acknowledge this fact, to employ any considerable number of colored men in the Faculties, and to seek the patronage of colored men of wealth and culture as advisers on the Board of Trustees, has led the colored alumni, and many friends of education, to feel that there is a *deep-seated cause* for this neglect of colored graduates; and that the explanation lies in caste prejudice. (p. 131)

Mrs. Mossell cites numerous arguments against blacks serving on the faculties of these institutions and soundly refutes each one. For instance, to disprove the argument that black men "would be unable to secure funds from the white pa-

trons of such institutions," she refers to the examples of Tuskegee Institute, Wilberforce University, and Livingston College (p. 131). Specifically, she cites Tuskegee as a successful case of the "Self-Education of the Negro": "I speak here of one large school which has been under Negro control from its inception, at which everything is done neatly, thoroughly, and with intelligent despatch" (p. 133).

The public debate of this issue centered around Howard, Lincoln, Hampton, and Biddle, institutions of higher education that were devoted exclusively to the education of blacks, but that did not hire black professors or administrators. Ironically, it was the white former abolitionists and Union officers on the trustee boards of these institutions who, in the words of Rev. Francis Grimké, "were diligently seeking to propagate the damnable heresy that it was immodest and presumptuous for black men to aspire to such positions" (p. 136).

Although Mrs. Mossell's essay speaks of the aspirations and qualifications of "colored men" to serve as college teachers, it is evident in the subtext of her argument that "colored women" in many cases are likewise qualified and "now thoroughly competent for such positions" (p. 131). This early argument for affirmative action in hiring blacks to college teaching positions exemplifies Mrs. Mossell's racial and sexual politics and her rhetorical strategies of subversion. In "Caste in Institutions," she employs a journalistic style and uses the technique of reportage to make her point, thus avoiding the accusation of immodesty on her own part. An editorial quoted from the *St. Joseph's Advocate* of Baltimore expresses her point of view: "If the equity of the well-worn balancer, *ceteris paribus* (all the other qualifications being on a par), be admitted, expressed or understood, then colored

men and women should have a preference in every colored institution. We go further, in non-essentials a slightly imperfect par should not amount to a perfect bar" (p. 138). For additional support, Mrs. Mossell also quotes such men as Frederick Douglass, Rev. Francis Grimké, and Dr. Nathan Francis Mossell (among others). Yet her vision for the advancement of black women is consistent with her vision of racial uplift. Her noble womanhood must develop in the context of a "growing race"; the "growing race" must, at the same time, allow for the development of "noble womanhood" and greater equality in home and family life.

The final section of *The Work* is composed entirely of Mrs. Mossell's original poetry and geared primarily toward a female audience. Sentimental titles include "Love's Promptings," "My Babes that Never Grow Old," and "Why Baby was Named Chris." Several of the poems are meant to advise and teach. An example is "Words":

> The threat of pain, and fear, and hate,
>   You shouted in your wrath,
> With all its deadly doing, still
>   Is lying in your path.
>
> Nay, e'en the tiny waves of air
>   Your secret will not keep,
> And all you speak when wide awake
>   Is whispered, though you sleep.
>
> A word may be a curse, a stab,
>   And, when the sun is west,
> Its onward course it still may run
>   And rankle in some breast.
>
> But words, small words, and yet how great,
>   Scarce do we heed their power;

> Yet they may fill the heart with joy,
>   And soften sorrow's hour.   (p. 158)

Though the rhyme and meter in this poem are traditional
and the message the standard stuff of the Victorian woman's
book, other poems are more race-conscious, if formally as
conservative. Examples include "The Martyrs of To-day,"
"Child of the Southland," and especially "Tell the North that
We are Rising":

> But we still would send the message
> To our friends where'er they roam,
> We are rising, yea, have risen:
> Future blessings yet will come.
>
> Noble son of noble mother,
> When our hearts would shrink and falter,
> We yet treasure up your message,
> Laying it on freedom's altar.
>
> We with courage strive to conquer,
> 'Till as England's Hebrews stand
> We are neither slaves nor tyrants,
> But are freemen on free land.   (p. 162)

Clearly Mrs. Mossell's most militant poetic statements focus
on the elevation of the black race—noble sons of noble mothers. Her feminist sentiments here take a secondary place to
the quest for freedom and literacy for all black people. The
combination of militant black poetry and sentimental "wom-
en's verse" strikes a balance acceptable to Mrs. Mossell's audience and transforms the "cult of the lady" into a race-
conscious black womanhood.

   The Work of the Afro-American Woman recorded the black
woman's moral, material, intellectual, and artistic progress

within the dominant culture of Victorian America. It held exemplary models of black womanhood before the public view, argued for an end to caste and color discrimination, and challenged the so-called "cult of true womanhood" with race-centered analysis.

For the contemporary reader, *The Work* represents a historical connection with the black foremothers who defended their names and images and documented their literary and cultural traditions at the turn of the century. In this work lie the wellsprings of black feminist literary expression and the same impulses to document, to share, to inspire and instruct that inform the writings of today's black women.

The Work of the Afro-American Woman should also be appreciated for its usefulness as a document of black American intellectual history, for time has proven Mrs. Mossell's assertion that "the intellectual history of a race is always of value in determining the past and future of it" (p. 49). "Every human attempt must have had its first, feeble, rudimentary steps, must have one day been the era of small things," she wrote. "The first tiny stream that at last swells to a broad river having therefore its own important place in the future life of that fact, so these faint, tottering intellectual steps must be worthy of record" (p. 49).

REFERENCES

Giddings, Paula. *When and Where I Enter: The Impact of Black Women on Race and Sex in America.* New York: William Morrow and Company, 1984.

Logan, Rayford W., and Winston, Michael R., eds. *The Dictionary of American Negro Biography.* New York: Norton and Company, 1982.

The Work of
the Afro-American Woman

THE WORK

OF THE

AFRO-AMERICAN WOMAN

BY

MRS. N. F. MOSSELL

SECOND EDITION

PHILADELPHIA
GEO. S. FERGUSON COMPANY
1908

INTRODUCTION.

IT is worthy of note as well as of congratulation that colored women are making great advancement in literary ventures.

In the year 1892 three books were given the world by this class of writers, well worthy of high consideration: Mrs. A. J. Cooper, "A Voice from the South by a Black Woman of the South;" Mrs. F. E. W. Harper, "Iola; or, Shadows Uplifted;" and Mrs. W. A. Dove, "The Life and Sermons of Rev. W. A. Dove."

Mrs. Mossell has continued this interesting list with THE WORK OF THE AFRO-AMERICAN WOMAN. When the women of any race become intelligent and active in literary pursuits, that race has acquired the greatest guarantee of success. This book will not only have that influence upon the world which comes from the consideration mentioned above, but, being thoughtfully prepared with a view to impressing a growing race with the importance of a correct life and independent thought, it must add largely to the educative cause of that race.

Mrs. Mossell has had large experience in the school room and in writing for the public press; hence has dealt largely with popular questions and studied closely the subjects treated in this book.

BENJAMIN F. LEE, D. D.,

Bishop of the A. M. E. Church.

DEDICATION.

To my two little daughters, Mary Campbell and Florence Alma Mossell, praying that they may grow into a pure and noble womanhood, this little volume is lovingly dedicated.

4

PREFACE.

IN the belief that some note of inspiration might be found in these writings for the budding womanhood of the race, they have been gathered and placed before it in this form. The author thanks her many readers for the kindly reception given her occasional work in the past, and bespeaks for this little volume the same generous reception in the present. She also desires to express her gratitude for helpful suggestions (in the preparation of this little book) from Mrs. F. E. W. Harper, Mrs. Bishop B. F. Lee, Miss Frazelia Campbell, T. Thomas Fortune, and Dr. N. F. Mossell. The author would be grateful to her readers if, by personal communication, they would make any correction or suggestion looking toward a more extended and revised edition of this work in the near future. Address

1432 Lombard Street,
PHILADELPHIA.

"To hold one's self in harmony with one's race while working out one's personal gift with freedom and conviction is to combine the highest results of inheritance and personal endeavor."

* * * * * * *

"The chief significance of this work is that it preserves for all time a chapter of humanity."

6

CONTENTS.

THE WORK OF THE AFRO-AMERICAN WOMAN.

"THE value of any published work, especially if historical in character, must be largely inspirational; this fact grows out of the truth that race instinct, race experience lies behind it, national feeling, or race pride always having for its development a basis of self-respect." The emancipation of the Negro race came about at the entrance to that which has been aptly termed the Woman's Century; co-education, higher education for women, had each gained a foothold. The "Woman's Suffrage" movement had passed the era of ridicule and entered upon that of critical study. The Woman's Christian Temperance Union had become a strong factor in the reform work of the nation. These facts made the uplifting of the womanhood of this race a more hopeful task than might otherwise have been, and gave to the individual woman of the race opportunities to reach a higher plane of development with less effort than would have been possible under a more unfavorable aspect of the woman question. Trammelled by their past condition and its consequent poverty, combined with the blasting influence of caste prejudice, they have yet made a fair showing.

The men of the race, in most instances, have been generous, doing all in their power to allow the women of the race to rise with them. "Woman's Work in America," by Anna Nathan Myer, garners up the grain from the harvest field of labor of our Anglo-American sisters. I would do for the women of my race, in a few words, this work that has been so ably done for our more favored sisters by another and abler pen. Accepting largely the divisions laid down in the above-mentioned volume, we have, along the line of successful educational work in the North, that most successful teacher and eloquent lecturer, Mrs. Fanny J. Coppin, principal of the Institute for Colored Youth at Philadelphia. Mrs. Coppin, one of the early graduates of Oberlin College, developed into one of the most noted educators in the United States. Hundreds of her graduates have filled positions of honor; hundreds of them are laboring as teachers for the upbuilding of their race. The grand work of establishing an Industrial School in connection with the Institute did not satisfy the heart of this noble benefactress of her race, but she at once set about establishing a boarding home for pupils from a distance. The effort is prospering and will no doubt be an assured fact in the near future. This lady is a very busy worker in various fields scores of needy students have been assisted by her own open-handed charity, as well as by the interest secured through her in their behalf. Her home is one of unostentatious hospitality.   Mrs. Coppin is the wife of Rev. Levi Coppin, D. D., editor of the A. M. E. Review.

Miss Julia Jones, Miss Lottie Bassett, and Miss Frazelia Campbell, of the same institution, Caroline R. Le Count of the O. V. Catto School, of Philadelphia, Mrs. S. S. Garnet, principal of Grammar School 81, 17th street, New York City, Edwina Kruse, principal of the Howard School, Wilmington, Del., are able educators.   In the East, we have Miss Maria Baldwin, principal of the Agassiz School, Cambridgeport, Mass. In the South, we have Mrs. Anna J. Cooper, of the High School, Washington, D. C., Prof. Mary V. Cook, Miss Bessie Cook, of Howard University, Miss Lucy Moten, principal of the Normal School of Washington, who was one of the honorary vice-presidents of the World's Educational Conference at the World's Fair, and Miss Mary Patterson; passing farther southward, Miss Lucy Laney, of the Haynes Industrial School at Augusta, Ga., Miss Alice Dugged Cary, and scores of others, who are doing good work.   Mrs. Wm. Weaver, who with her husband is laboring against great odds in the upbuilding of the Gloucester Industrial School, Va., deserves honorable mention.   In the West, we ɩɩave successful teachers giving instruction to our own race ; we have also several Afro-American women elected to teacherships in the white schools of Cleveland, placed there as one must readily see by unquestioned merit. Miss Jennie Enola Wise, of the State Normal School, Alabama, now Mrs. Dr. H. T. Johnson, wife of the editor of The Christian Recorder, Miss Anna Jones, of Wilberforce, Miss Ione Wood and Miss Lucy Wilmot Smith, of the Kentucky State Normal School, have all labored successfully at their chosen profession. Among eminent educators who have retired from active work in this field of effort we would mention Miss Pet Kiger, now Mrs. Isaiah Wears, Mrs. Silone Yates, formerly of Lincoln Institute, Mrs. Cordelia Atwell, Mrs. Susie Shorter, Mrs. Dr. Alston of Asheville, N. C., formerly of Shaw University, Mrs. Sarah Early, of Wilberforce University, Mrs. Wm. D. Cook, formerly Miss Bertha Wolf, of Allen University. Miss Florence Cozzen and Miss Fanny Somerville of Philadelphia are successful kindergartners. Very many of the higher grade institutions for the education of Afro-American students North, South, East and West employ in their corps of teachers women of the race who are doing able work on the basis of education received in the High and Normal Schools of the various States. Our girls are yearly entering the collegiate institutions of the land,

We can boast of Ella Smith, of Newport, an M. A. of Wellesley. Anna J. Cooper, Fanny J. Coppin and Mary Church Terril, of Oberlin. Wilberforce, Atlanta, Fisk, Howard, Scotia, Shaw, Tuskegee, Livingstone. The Institute for Colored Youth at Philadelphia, Wayland Seminary and Hampton are graduating yearly a fair share of the successful educators in this country, and continue to enroll yearly those who will in later years do honor to their race.

Miss Florence and Miss Cordelia Ray, Miss Mary Eato and Miss Imogene Howard have all secured the degree of master of Pedagogy from the University of New York; Miss Mollie Durham and Miss Annie Marriot of Philadelphia have secured Supervising Principals' certificates in that city.

Have the women of this race yet made a record in literature ? We believe that we can answer this question in the affirmative. Phyllis Wheatley, our first authoress, gave to the world a most creditable volume of poems. The beautiful verses of the little slave girl, who though a captive yet sung her song of freedom, are still studied with interest.

The path of literature open to our women with their yet meagre attainments has been traveled to some purpose by Mrs. Frances Ellen Watkins Harper, who has through a long widowhood sustained herself and her family by her pen and by her voice as a lecturer on

the reforms of the hour.   Mrs. Harper is the author of
two volumes of poems, " Forest Leaves " and " Moses."
A novel, " Iola Leroy, or, The Shadows Uplifted,"
from the pen of this gifted woman, has just been
placed upon the market.   As superintendent of the
colored work in the " Woman's Christian Temperance
Union " she has labored for years with great success.
A member of the " National Council of Women," of
the " Association for the Advancement of Women,"
of the " Colored Authors and Educators Association,"
she has at various meetings of these societies furnished
valuable papers ; " Dependent Races " and " Enlight-
ened Motherhood " being especially worthy of mention.   The N. Y. Independent, A. M. E. Review,
and other high grade journals receive contributions
from her pen.   Mrs. Anna J. Cooper, author of " A
Voice from the South by a Black Woman of the
South," has given to the world one of the finest contributions yet made toward the solution of the Negro
problem.   Mrs. Josephine Heard is the author of
" Morning Glories," a charming little volume of verse.
Mrs. M. A. Dove, the widow of Rev. W. A. Dove, is
the author of a biographical sketch of her late husband that has received unstinted praise.   " Poor Ben,"
a biographical sketch of the life of Benjamin F. Ar-
nett, D. D., by Lucretia Coleman, and a volume of
poems by Mrs. Frankie Wassoms, continues our list of

fair authors. Mrs. Harvey Johnson, wife of Dr. Harvey Johnson, of Baltimore, Md., has published two valuable Sabbath School stories, for which she has received a good round sum; they are both published and have been purchased by the American Baptist Publication Society of Philadelphia.   Amanda Smith, the noted evangelist, has published a most interesting auto-biography of her labors in Africa, England, and the United States.

Miss Florence and H. Cordelia Ray are the authors of an exquisite memorial volume in honor of their father, the late Charles B. Ray, of New York City. "Aunt Lindy," a story from the pen of Mrs. Wm. E. Matthews, president of the Women's Loyal Union of Brooklyn, N. Y., is our latest contribution to author-ship. Mrs. Matthews is widely known by her chosen nom de plume "Victoria Earle."

In Journalism.

The sex and race have reached high-water marks through the editorship of "Free Speech," by Ida B. Wells; "Ringwood's Magazine," Mrs. Julia Costen; "St. Matthew's Lyceum Journal," Mrs. M. E. Lambert; "Virginia Lancet," Lucindia Bragg; "The Boston Courant" and "Woman's Era," Mrs. Josephine Ruffin; "The Musical Messenger," Miss Tillman; and "Wo-man's Light and Love," a journal of Home and Foreign

Missions, published at Harrisburg, Pa., by Mrs. Lida Lowry and Mrs. Emma Ransom.

Victoria Earle of Waverly's Magazine, Lillian A. Lewis of the Boston Herald, Florence A. Lewis having charge of editorial departments of Golden Days and the Philadelphia Press, show unerringly the value of our women's work in this line of effort. Miss Frazelia Campbell's translations from the German give her high rank in this field of work.

Mrs. Mary E. Lee, wife of Bishop B. F. Lee, Miss Mary Britton, Mrs. Layton, of Los Angeles, Mrs. Alice Felts, wife of Rev. Cethe Felts, Anna E. Geary, Elizabeth Frazier, Frances Parker, M. E. Buckner, Mattie F. Roberts, Ada Newton Harris, Bella Dorce, H. A. Rice, Josephine Turpin, Washington, Katie D. Yankton, Lucy Wilmot Smith, Cordelia Ray, Lucinda Bragg, Fannie C. Bently, Mrs. Fannie Barrier Williams, Kate Tillman, Mrs. Silone Yates, Florida Ridley, Medora Gould, Miss Dora J. Cole, Irene DeMortie, Maria Ridley, M. Elizabeth Johnson, Leslie Wilmot, Alice Ruth Moore, Mrs. Susie Shorter, Mrs. Mollie Church Terril, Miss Virginia Whitsett, Dr. Alice Woodby McKane, Dr. Lucy Hughes Brown, Maritcha Lyons, Mrs. Majors, Mrs. Scruggs, and Mrs. I. Garland Penn, have done good work in the past, and in many cases are still doing such work in literary lines as must reflect high honor on their race and sex.

The profession of medicine has proven more attractive, and more lucrative also, to Afro-American women than either of the other liberal professions.   We have some dozen graduates of the finest institutions in the country; among the earliest is Dr. Susan McKinney, a graduate of the Women's Medical College of N. Y.; having been a student under Dr. Clement Lozier is largely to the advantage of Dr. McKinney. As a member of the Medical Staff of the Women's Dispensary and of the City Society of Homœopathy the Doctor is doing efficient work; this combined with a large and rapidly growing practice makes her labors along race efforts especially worthy of commendation. Dr. R. J. Cole and Dr. Caroline V. Anderson were the pioneers from the Phila. Women's Medical College; Dr. Cole is also an excellent German scholar.   Dr. Anderson, although not an author in her own right, yet gave valuable assistance to her father, Wm. Still, Esq., in the preparation of his famous work " The Underground Railroad." Dr. Anderson conducts a Dispensary in connection with the mission work of the Berean Presbyterian Church, South College Ave.,Phila.,of which her husband, the Rev. Matthew Anderson, is pastor. The doctor has secured through the kindness of wealthy friends an additional aid to the work of this mission by the gift of a cottage at Mt. Pleasant to be used as a retreat for invalids.   Dr. Verina Morton is practising in

2

partnership with her husband, an eminent physician of Brooklyn, N. Y. Dr. Alice Woodby McKane was resident physician at the Haynes Normal and Industrial School until her marriage with Dr. McKane. She has lately organized a Nurses' Training School at Savannah, Ga. Dr. Hallie Tanner Johnson, the eldest daughter of Bishop B. T. Tanner of the A. M. E. Church, is resident physician at Tuskegee University, Ala. This lady had the honor of being the first woman of any race to practise medicine in the State of Alabama. She has since entering upon her work at Tuskegee established a Nurses' Training School and Dispensary at that institution. The Doctor has lately become the wife of Prof. John Quincy Johnson, President of Allen University. Dr. Alice Bennett, of the Women's Medical College, is pleasantly located in the East. Dr. Consuelo Clark, a graduate of the Cincinnati Medical College, is an eminently successful practitioner. Dr. Georgiana Rumly, deceased, was a recent graduate of Howard University. Meharry Medical College, Nashville, Tenn., has two female graduates, Dr. Georgia L. Patton of the class of 93, now an independent Medical Missionary at Monrovia, Liberia, and Dr. Lucinda D. Key, class of 94, a successful practitioner at Chattanooga, Tenn. Dr. Lucy Hughes Brown, the latest graduate we have to record in this honorable profession, is now an alumnus of the Women's Medical College, Philadelphia,

Dr. Brown has entered upon an excellent practice at Wilmington, N. C. Miss L. C. Fleming, who has labored very efficiently as a missionary in South Africa, has entered upon her medical course at the above institution. We have in the profession of pharmacy, three graduates of Meharry Medical College, these ladies having taken their degrees at this year's Commencement, Miss Matilda Lloyd, of Nashville, Tenn., Miss Margaret A. Miller, of S. C., and, Miss Bella B. Coleman, who has entered a drug store at Natchez, Miss.

Dr. Ida Gray, our only known graduate in dentistry, hails from the University at Mich., receiving her degree in 1890. Dr. Gray at once entered upon her work and has found herself highly appreciated. The Doctor has a charming personality.

We have as trained nurses Mrs. Minnie Hogan, of the Nurses' Training School of the University of Pa., Miss Annie Reeve and Mrs. Nicholson of the Women's Medical College, Mrs. Georgian Rumbly, lately deceased, took a Nurse's course at Howard University and practised this profession prior to entering upon a Medical course.

We have in the profession of law three graduates, Mrs. Mary Shadd Cary, of Washington, D. C., Miss Florence Ray, of N.Y., and Miss Ida Platt, of Chicago. The first named is also an eloquent lecturer the second an author of merit. Miss Ida B. Platt, of Chicago, has the honor of being the only representative of the race now practising at the bar. Miss Platt is a native of Chicago, a graduate of the High School of that city, at the early age of sixteen she had finished the course taking first rank among the students of that institution. At a later date this studious young lady entered an insurance office acting in the capacity of stenographer and private secretary where the correspondence required proficiency in the German and French languages. In 1892 she entered a prominent law office as stenographer and at a later date she established an independent office of law reporting and stenography, (Germans as it must be said to their credit in this as in most similiar cases giving the largest percentage of patronage received from the dominant race). Two years ago Miss Platt entered the Chicago Law School from which she has recently graduated with the exceedingly creditable average of 96. This lady deserves unstinted praise for her courage and perseverance. Busy at her usual work during the day she had only the evening hours in which to pursue her chosen profession and yet ranked among the best students of her class.

No woman of the race has completed a theological course so far as we can learn, but large numbers inspired with zeal for the Master's kingdom have gone forth to evangelistic and mission work. Amanda Smith, **now** laboring in Canada, spent many months with Bishop Taylor in the opening up of his mission work in Africa.

Perhaps it might be said we have done the least in the line of State work and yet we believe, that according to the opportunities accorded us we have done our share. In time of war, in famine, in time of fire or flood, and especially during the horrors of pestilence the women of this race have done noble work often calling forth public praise; as was the case at Memphis, a few years ago, when the mayor of that city complimented the women of the race for the kindness to the sufferers in the awful epidemic that had recently visited that district.

In the East and West, on the School and local option question they have given able support, in local and ward charity they have always done their share of the work in hand. Miss Amelia Mills, of Philadelphia, has been for years a most efficient worker especially along the line of the Country Week Association.

During the World's Fair we had five experienced refined and cultivated women upon the World's Fair State Committees, Miss Imogene Howard, of N. Y., Mrs. Fannie Barrier Williams, of Chicago, who read a most able paper before the World's Parliament of Religions, Miss Florence A. Lewis, of Philadelphia, who was also World's Fair correspondent for the Philadelphia Times.   Mrs. S. A. Williams, of New Orleans and Mrs. M. A. Curtis, of Chicago.

Along the line of Art we have one noble representative : the work of Edmonia Lewis, the sculptress, is so well known that it scarce needs repetition ; her " Cleopatra Dying," exhibited at the Centennial Exhibition, received a medal of honor.   Most of her works have been sold to titled persons of Europe.   Elizabeth Greenfield Selika, Flora Batson Bergen, Madame Sisseretta Jones, Madame Saville Jones, Madame Nellie Brown Mitchell, Madame Dessiro Plato, Mrs. Lizzie Pugh Dugan, and Miss Agnes Tucker rank as the Pattis and Nilssons of the race.   In many cases not only delighting the millions of the common people, but receiving marked tokens of appreciation from the crowned heads of the European nations, Hallie Quinn Brown, Ednorah Nahr, Henrietta Vinton Davis, Alice Franklin, now Mrs. T. McCants Stewart, Mary Harper, Matilda Herbert and Emma White take rank among the finest elocutionists of the United States.   As accomplished pianists we have Madame Montgomery, Madame Williams, Mrs. Ida Gilbert Chestnut, Miss Inez Casey and Mrs. Cora Tucker Scott.   The women of this race have always been industrious, however much the traducers of the race may attempt to make it appear otherwise. They are proving daily the truth of this assertion.

The following word of praise from a recent writer, in the "Boston Transcript," voices this self evident truth as set forth in the present condition of the most humble of our women, laboring in the South-land. This writer in the closing lines of an exceptionally truthful article entitled, "The Southern Plantation of To day," gives this tribute to the Afro-American woman of this section of our fair land. "Too much credit cannot be given these hard-working wives and mothers, who hoe, rake, cook, wash, chop, patch and mend, from morning until night; very often garments will be patched until scarcely a trace of the original foundation material can be seen, and there are many cases where the wife is much the best 'cotton chopper' of the two, and her work far more desirable than her husband's. The wife works as hard as her husband—harder in fact, because when her field work is over she cooks the simple meals, washes the clothes, and patches the garments for her numerous family by the blaze of a lightwood torch after the members of the household are rolled in their respective 'quilts' and voyaging in slumberland. She does more than this, for she raises chickens and turkeys, sometimes geese and ducks, using the eggs for pocket money."

The women of this race have been industrious but it is only in late years, that they have reaped the fruits of their own industry. Many have built up businesses for themselves that net thousands of dollars. Mrs. Henrietta Dutērte, the oldest and most successful undertaker of color in Philadelphia, is a brilliant example, Mrs. Addison Foster is also a successful worker in this field of effort.

Mrs. Winnie Watson of Louisville is a graduate of the Clark School of embalming. She graduated in a class of forty-five, three colored and forty-two white, and yet took first honor. She has entered into partnership with her husband who is an undertaker.

Mrs. Caroline E. White is a retired dry goods merchant of Philadelphia. Mrs. Margaret Jones, cateress, and many of our women in the Eastern and Western States having handsome millinery, dressmaking, and hair dressing parlors, carried on successfully attest the business capacity of the Afro-American woman. For years the finest tonsorial parlor on the Pacific coast, was owned and conducted by a woman of the race. As managers of the finest grade of hotels, they have been a marked success.

It is stated on the authority of numbers of reputable journals, that in the camp at Yasoo, Montana, a colored woman named Millie Ringold ran the first hotel at that place and established an enviable reputation as a prospector and also, that Mrs. C. Whetzel, a resident of St. John, New Brunswick, becoming wid-

owed in early life continued the ice trade formerly
carried on by her husband. She first secured a long
lease on the only body of fresh water within city limits
with this advantage secured she placed the whole business on a secure footing, providing all modern
improvements to secure the desired end, and at present
has the monopoly of this business in that city.
Of late years she has invented an ice house, whereby
meats and other provisions may be kept for months
without losing their sweetness.

As stenographers, type writers, book keepers, and
sales women those of the race who have gained a
foothold in these employments have never failed to
give satisfaction.

Mrs. M. E. Elliot years ago secured a patent on
several toilet articles and opened branch establishments
in many cities.

A colored woman has a contract for hauling sand at
a small town in Florida.   In connection with this work
she carries on a small farm and poultry yard gaining
thereby more than a comfortable living for herself and
family. Miss Maud Benjamin, of Washington, has
patented a call bell. Mrs. N. F. Mossell, of Phila.,
has invented a camping table and portable kitchen.
Many unique inventions are now in the possession of
Afro-American women too poor to secure patents.

That the women of this race did not lack force of

character, was shown at an early day, when Elizabeth Freemen, popularly known as " Mum Bett," and Jennie Slew of Ipswich sued for their liberty under the Bill of Rights, both winning their cases.

It is also on record that Deborah Gannet, who had enlisted during the Revolutionary war in Captain Wells' company, under the name of Robert Shurtliffe, serving from May, 1782, until October 23, 1783, discharged the duties of her office and at the same time, preserved inviolate the virtue of her sex, and was granted therefore a pension of thirty-four pounds.

" ' Happy ' or Kate Ferguson, born a slave, opened a Sunday School in Dr. John Mason's Murray Street Church, in New York City, in 1774. She secured homes for forty-eight children, white and black. The school growing, the lecture room was opened, Dr. Mason and his teachers assisting ' Happy ' in her work." So says Colored American, a book printed through a fund bequeathed by Lindley Murray, " to promote piety, virtue and the truths of Christianity." This was the beginning of the Sunday School in Murray Street Church, and Kate Ferguson, the colored woman who had been a slave is believed to have thus gathered the first Sunday School in New York City. Says W. E. Chandler in his history of the Sabbath Schools of New York City, after stating the above facts, " God bless the dusky hands that broke here an alabaster box, the perfume of which still lingers about the great metropolis."

We have in the line of musical composers, Miss Estelle Rickets, Miss Bragg, Miss Tillman, Mrs. Yeocum and Mrs. Ella Mossell. In artistic work, Miss Julia F. Jones, Mrs. Parker Denny and Miss Nelson, now an art student of Philadelphia, take rank with those who are doing successful work. Miss Ida Bowser is a graduate of the Musical Department of the University of Pennsylvania. We have also several graduates of the Boston Conservatory of Music. The New York Conservatory has also several of our girls as pupils; Miss Blanche D. Washington is a student in harmony and composition. Madame Thurber's invitation and Prof. Dvorak's statement that the future music of this country must be founded upon what are called Negro melodies, has given great encouragement to the young of the race who are ambitious musically. Of late years the dramatic instinct has developed sufficiently to enable the presentation of many of the best plays. The Afro-American woman taking her part therein with an ease and grace that astonishes those who go to mock her efforts. Perhaps the effort that is most unique and yet entirely consistent with the character of the race has been done along the line of philanthropic work. Within these later years since better opportunities for educational and industrial work have been opened to them in the more favored sections of the country; many of our women have turned aside from laboring for their individual success and given thought to the condition of the weak and suffering classes. They have shown that the marvellous loving kindness and patience that is recorded of the native women of Africa, by Mungo Park, the great African explorer, that forms the tie that still holds captive to this day the heart of the white foster child of the "black mammies" of the Southland was not crushed out by the iron heel of slavery but still wells up in their bosoms and in this brighter day overflows in compassion for the poor and helpless of their own down-trodden race.

Two of the earliest laborers in this field of effort were "Moses" and "Sojourner Truth," Harriet, known for many years as "Moses," was a full blooded African woman, who escaped from slavery on the Eastern shore of Maryland. She returned to the South nineteen times, carrying off four hundred slaves. Gov. Andrew of Massachusetts, sent her as a scout and spy with the union army during the war; at its close she labored for the soldiers in the hospitals and later with the "Freedmen's Bureau," she is now living at Auburn, N. Y., where she looks after the poor and infirm of her race. "Sojourner Truth" was born in Webster County, N. Y., she escaped from slavery and labored for years in the Anti-Slavery, Woman's Suffrage and Temperance movements. She was a woman of magnificient presence, great power and magnetism. She possessed at her death a book called by her, the "Book of Life," it contained kind words and thoughts for her from the great of every land. Mrs. Mary Ella Mossell, wife of Rev. C. W. Mossell, labored with her husband for eight years at Port Au Prince, Hayti, establishing at that point a mission school for girls. Mrs. Mossell died in America two years after her return to their home at Baltimore, Md. The school is a portion of the work of Foreign Missions of the A. M. E. Church, and has been named the Mossell Mission School in honor of its deceased founder.

Miss Elizabeth Ralls, the organizer of the "Sarah Allen Mission and Faith Home," of Philadelphia, is a remarkable character. Without education or wealth, with a heart overflowing with love to the poor, she has from childhood, labored in season and out of season in the mission cause. For many years she served a Christmas dinner to the poor of her race, in Philadelphia, over five hundred being present. Boxes of clothing and food were distributed monthly. Of late years she has rented a house and taken in the aged who could not gain admittance to other institutions. She takes her basket on her arm and goes to the market, gleaning for her poor. The whole work is carried on by faith. Her sweet, loving countenance, the "darlings" and "dovies" that drop from her lips as she places the hands on one's shoulder and looks lovingly into the eyes of the person addressed carries conviction. Her coffers are always filled to the extent of the actual need of "her poor people," as she calls them. Mrs. Sarah Gorham is now a laborer in Africa under the Women's Mite Missionary Society of the A. M. E. Church. Mission work has also been done in the South by Miss Lucy Laney, of Augusta, Ga., and Miss Alice Dugged Cary, Mrs. Lynch, and Mrs. McClean, in the West and Southwest are doing good work. Mrs. S. A. Williams, of New Orleans, has organized an orphanage which is succeeding. Mrs. Mary Barboza, a daughter of the late Henry Highland Garnet, late consul to Liberia, sacrificed her life laboring to establish a school for girls in Liberia. Mrs. Roberts, widow of ex-president Roberts, of Liberia, is laboring to establish a hospital for girls at that point. Mrs. Fanny Barrier Williams has co-operated with a corps of physicians in establishing a hospital and Nurses' Training School in Chicago. Mrs. Maria Shorter, wife of Bishop James Shorter, of the A. M. E. Church, by a large contribution, assisted in the opening of Wilberforce College. Mrs. Olivia Washington, the deceased wife of Prof. Booker Washington, of

Tuskegee Industrial School, did much by her labors to place that institution on a secure footing. Mrs. I. Shipley, of Camden, N. J., has established a Faith Retreat at Asbury Park ; she also does much mission work in her native city. Misses Fanny and Alma Somerville, of Philadelphia, are quiet but efficient mission workers, especially along the line of Working Girls' Clubs. Miss Planter, a wealthy lady of color, gave a large bequest to Livingstone College, N. C. Mrs. Catherine Teagle and Mrs. Harriet Hayden both bequeathed handsome sums to the cause of Afro-American education. Mrs. Stephen Smith and Mrs. Mary A. Campbell, wife of Bishop J. P. Campbell, and Mrs. Margaret Boling have given largely of their means and labors toward the establishment of the Old Folks' Home at Philadelphia. Miss Nettie Wilmer, who has done efficient mission work in various lines, is now laboring for the upbuilding of the Gloucester Industrial School, Va.

The Lend a Hand, Christian Endeavor, Epworth League and like institutions have a large contingent of our women as efficient workers. The last effort at organized work by the womanhood of this race has been the organization of two associations, namely, the Woman's Loyal Union of Brooklyn and New York, and the Colored Woman's League, of Washington, D. C. These associations have for their work the collecting of statistics and facts showing the moral, intellectual, industrial, and social growth and attainments of Afro-Americans. They aim to foster unity of purpose, to consider and determine the methods that will promote the best interests of the Afro-American race, to bring into active fellowship and organic union all movements which may be classed under the head of Woman's Work. It is also their intention to receive and distribute information concerning the activities of Afro-Americans throughout the length and breadth of the land.

Perhaps the greatest work in philanthropy yet accomplished by any woman of the race is that undertaken and so successfully carried out at the present hour by Miss Ida B. Wells.

This lady is a native of Holly Springs, Miss. She received a liberal education for the greater part at Rust University. A teacher for a few months in the State of Arkansas, she at a later date became a resident and teacher at Memphis, Tenn. This position she held for some seven years. Criticism of the condition of affairs prevailing in the colored school of Memphis gained the lady the ill-will of the Board of Education, and at the following term she failed to receive an appointment.

Miss Wells, nothing daunted, purchased a one-third interest in the Memphis *Free Speech*. The paper was much benefited by this fact and continued to be an eminent success from every point of view.

March 9, 1892, occurred at Memphis (in a section of the town called the Curve) a most brutal and out-rageous lynching of Afro-Americans. An attempt was made by the press of Memphis to justify this crime by the most flagrantly untruthful statements regarding the conduct of the men lynched.

Miss Wells at once began in *Free Speech* a series of letters and editorials setting forth the true state of the case. These editorials were succeeded by a series of articles criticising and condemning the treatment of her race in Memphis.

At a later date, during the month of May, 1892, there appeared in the columns of *Free Speech* an editorial from the pen of our heroine that has since become famous.

Starting out on a visit to Oklahoma and later to New York City, Miss Wells stopped in Philadelphia on a visit to Mrs. F. E. W. Harper and to take a peep at the doings of the A. M. E. General Conference then in session at that city. What was her consternation to find letters pouring in upon her from friends and correspondents at Memphis warning her not to return to her office on pain of being lynched. She was in-formed that her newspaper plant had been destroyed and the two male editors had been forced to flee for their lives.

Miss Wells was at once placed upon the staff of the

3

New York *Age*, and in the issue of that paper of June 27, 1892, gave the facts that led to the suspension of her paper and the real motive for Lynch and Mob Law.

In the early fall Miss Wells entered upon a lecturing tour among her own race in the United States; later a committee of ladies under the title of The Woman's Loyal Union of Brooklyn and New York gave her a grand reception, a testimonial purse of $400 and also a beautiful gold pen engraved with the legend "Mizpah."

Miss Wells continued her lecturing tour meeting with a hearty welcome, especially in the city of Boston. The press of that city gave her a flattering reception, publishing lengthy interviews and carefully reporting her addresses. Mrs. Josephine Ruffin, of the Boston *Courant*, used her influence to get Miss Wells's cause a hearing before the most exclusive Women's Clubs of Boston and with great success. The Moral Educational Association, of Boston, was of this number.

The ire of the Memphis press was aroused by the courtesy shown Miss Wells at Boston, and retaliated by flooding the North with slanderous accusations against the martyr editor.

During the late fall Miss Wells was visited at Philadelphia by Miss Catherine Impey, of London, England, editor of *Anti-Caste*. By this lady's invitation

Miss Wells sailed to England in the spring to present her cause to the reform element of English society. She lectured on " Lynch Law," in England and Scotland, for many weeks, speaking at forty meetings in most of the prominent cities of England and Scotland. At Glasgow, London, Liverpool, Edinburg, Aberdeen, Huntley, Morningside, Manchester, Carruter's Close, and many other points, she was heartily welcomed by the best people ; great interest in the cause she represented was thereby aroused. This interest culminated in the formation of an important society.

In the drawing-room of Mrs. Isabella Favie Mayo, April 21, 3 P. M., 1893, at Aberdeen, Scotland, with Miss Wells, Miss Catherine Impey and Dr. George Fernands, together with fifty of the most prominent clergy, professionals, tradesmen and others, was put in operation a force that will tell on the life of unborn generations. A second meeting was held later on at Music Hall, Aberdeen, April 24th. Professor Iverach offered a resolution condemnatory of lynching, which was seconded by Rev. James Henderson, the son of an ex-Mayor of this city.

The society formed received the name of " The Society for the Recognition of the Brotherhood of Man." Its aims were stated in the following declaration :—

(*a*) The Society for the Recognition of the Brotherhood of Man declares itself fundamentally opposed to the system of race separation, by which the despised members of a community are cut off from the social, civil, and religious life of their fellow-men.

(*b*) It regards lynching and other forms of brutal injustice inflicted on the weaker communities of the world as having their root in Race Prejudice, which is directly fostered by the estrangement and lack of sympathy consequent on Race Separation.

(*c*) This Society for the Recognition of the Brotherhood of Man therefore requires its members to refrain from all complicity in the system of Race Separation, whether as individuals, or by co-membership in organizations which tolerate and provide the same.

And those becoming members gave the following pledge:—

I, the undersigned, promise to help in securing to every member of the human family, *Freedom, Equal Opportunity* and *Brotherly Consideration*.

The publication * *Fraternity*, into which *Anti-Caste*

---

* In view of the recent death of S. J. Celestine Edwards, editor of *Fraternity*, the Society for the Recognition of the Brotherhood of Man have considered it advisable to declare that publication no longer the official organ of the society.

had been merged, became the organ of the Society, and S. J. Celestine Edwards was appointed editor.

Miss Eliza Wigham, Secretary of the Anti-Slavery Society, entertained Miss Wells during this visit.

Miss Wells soon after returned to the States, established herself in Chicago, and as a staff contributor to *The Conservator* and New York *Age* did valuable work that led to a wide-spread discussion of the subject of lynching of Afro-Americans in the Southland. Soon after she began the preparation of a pamphlet entitled " The Reason Why," for distribution at the World's Fair. This was a most carefully prepared series of papers on race subjects by such writers as the Hon. Fred. Douglass, I. Garland Penn, F. L. Barnett and Ida B. Wells.

Miss Wells was sent by the *Inter-Ocean* to secure the facts concerning a lynching case; these facts she secured and the result of her work was published in the columns of that influential journal.

Soon after, a few hours before the lynching of Lee Walker, at Memphis, Tenn., the following telegram was sent to the *Inter-Ocean*, Chicago:—

"MEMPHIS, July 22.

" To *Inter-Ocean*, Chicago:—Lee Walker, colored man, accused of ——, to be taken out and burned by whites. Can you send Miss Ida Wells to write it up? Answer.   R. M. MARTIN, with *Pub. Ledger*."

Miss Wells did much effective work for the race at the World's Fair. At its close she was soon after invited to again lecture in England under the auspices of " The Society for the Recognition of the Brotherhood of Man," which she had been instrumental in forming at her previous visit.

On February 28, 1894, Miss Wells once more sailed for the shores of " Old England."   While making her second lecturing tour, under the auspices of the above-named Society, resolutions endorsing her mission were secured from the following associations: The Congregational Union, National Baptist Association, Young Men's Christian Association, National British Women's Temperance Association, Women's Liberal Association, Society of Friends, Society for the Union of Churches, and the Unitarian Conference.

Lady Jeune, Mrs. Lockhart Smith, Charles F. Aked, Sir Edward Russell, and other prominent persons and members of the nobility opened their drawing-rooms to a favored few to listen to the story of the woes of Afro-Americans as recited by Miss Wells.   Sir Joseph Pease presided at the parliamentary breakfast given in Miss Wells' honor.

Miss Ellen Richards, who so many years ago had purchased the freedom of Frederick Douglass and Wm. Wells Brown, received our young philanthropist as her honored guest,

The following clipping from one of Miss Wells' letters to the New York *Age* will give an excellent idea of the drift of the public meetings held by her in London :—

The Rev. C. F. Aked (Liverpool) moved: "That this union, having learned with grief and horror of the wrongs done to the colored people of the Southern States of America by lawless mobs, expresses the opinion that the perpetuation of such outrages, unchecked by the civil power, must necessarily reflect upon the administration of justice in the United States and upon the honor of its people. It therefore calls upon all lovers of justice, of freedom, and of brotherhood in the churches of the United States, to demand for every citizen of the Republic, accused of crime, a proper trial in the courts of law." He said that the scandal he referred to had no parallel in the history of the world, and it was their duty as Christians to do their best to put a stop to it. In the Southern States of America there are 25,000 negro teachers in elementary schools, 500 negro preachers trained in the theological institutes of the people themselves, and 2500 negro preachers who had not received college training. The colored race had also produced 300 lawyers, 400 doctors, 200 newspapers, and they possessed property valued at £50,000,000 sterling. Yet these people are being whipped, scourged, hanged, flayed, and roasted at the stake. There had been 1000 lynchings within the last ten years, and the average now was from 150 to 200 every year. Some of these murders were foul beyond expression and such as to appall and disgrace humanity. Most of the lynchings were alleged to be for assaults upon women, but only a small proportion of cases were really of that kind. The mobs who lynched these poor people were generally drunk and half insane and always bestial. The church must not keep silent while the press spoke out, and he was glad to see that the *Daily Chronicle* was doing splendid service in the cause of humanity—(cheers)—called attention to the subject that morning, and told them to give a moral nudge to their American brethren. It was the duty of great nations to shame each other, and if they could do any good, he should be pleased. He appealed to them to prove by their action the solidarity of the human race and the brotherhood of man under the fatherhood of God, and thus to further the interest of the kingdom of heaven. (Cheers.)

Rev. Charles F. Aked was one of Miss Wells' ablest English supporters, and gave an excellent account of her work in the *Review of the Churches.*

Speaking of the purpose to be served by Miss Wells' mission to England, Mr. Aked says:—

" One thing she has set herself to do, and that there

seems to be every possibility of her accomplishing.

.   .   .   .   .   .

Miss Wells does not suppose that any direct political action can be taken, but she does suppose that British opinion, if aroused, can influence American press and pulpit, and through the press and pulpit the people of the Northern States."

The Anti-Lynching Committee formed in England has just given to the world through the publication of a letter from Miss Florence Balgarnie in the August 23d issue of the New York *Age* a list of its members. The men and women who in the name of humanity and civilization have banded themselves together in this committee are still adding both British and Americans to their numbers.   Among those who have already joined are :—

The Right Honorable the Duke of Argyle, K. G., K. T.; the Rev. C. F. Aked, Liverpool; Mr. W. Allan, M. P., Gateshead-on-Tyne; Mr. Wm. E. A. Axon, Manchester; the Rev. R. Armstrong, Liverpool; Mr. Thomas Burt, M. P., Morpeth; the Right Honorable Jacob Bright, M. P., Manchester; Mrs. Jacob Bright; Mr. Wm. Byles, M. P., Bradford; Mrs. Byles, Bradford; Mr. W. Blake-Odgers, Mr. E. K. Blyth, Mr. Percy Bunting, Mrs. Percy Bunting, Mr. Herbert Burrows, Mr. Bertram, Miss Bertram, Mr. P. W. Clayden, Mrs. P. W. Clayden, Mr. James G. Clarke,

the Rev. Dr. John Clifford, London; Sir Charles
Cameron, Bart., M. P., Glasgow; Mr. Francis A. Chan-
ning, M. P., Southampton; the Rev. Estlin Carpenter,
Oxford; Mr. Moncure D. Conway, Mrs. Conway,
U. S. A. and London; Mrs. E. T. Cook, London;
Mr. Wm. Crosfield, M. P., Liverpool; Mrs. J. Pass-
more Edwards, London; Mr. C. Diamond, M. P.,
Monaghan, N.; Mr. T. E. Ellis, M. P., Nottingham;
Mr. A. E. Fletcher, London; Miss Isabella Ford,
Leeds; the Right Honorable Sir T. Eldon Gorst,
M. P., Cambridge University; Mr. Frederic Harrison;
Mr. Justin McCarthy, M. P., Longford, N.; Mr.
Dadabhai Naoroji, M. P., India and London; the
Rev. Dr. Newman Hall, the Rev. Dr. Robert Horton,
Mr. T. A. Lang, London; Miss Kate Riley, South-
port; Lady Stevenson, London; Dr. Spence Watson,
Mrs. Spence Watson, Gateshead-on-Tyne; Mr. J. A.
Murray Macdonald, M. P., Mr. Tom Mann, London;
the Rev. Dr. W. F. Moulton, Cambridge; Sir Joseph
Pease, Bart., M. P., Durham; Sir Hugh Gilzen Reid,
Birmingham; Mrs. Henry Richardson, York; Sir
Edward Russell, Liverpool; Mr. Sapara, Africa and
London; Mr. C. P. Scott, Manchester; Professor James
Stuart, M. P., Mrs. Stuart, London; Mr. Charles
Schwann, M. P., Manchester; Miss Sharman-Craw-
ford, Ulster; the Rev. Canon Shuttleworth, London;
the Rev. S. Alfred Steinthal, Manchester; Mrs. Stan-

ton-Blatch, U. S. A. and Basingstoke; Alderman
Ben Tillett, London; Mr. John Wilson, M. P., Glasgow; the Rev. Philip Wicksteed, Mrs. Wicksteed,
London; Mr. Alfred Webb, M. P., Waterford, W.;
Mr. S. D. Wade, London; Mr. Mark Whitwill, Bris-
tol; Miss Eliza Wigham, Edinburgh; Mr. Wm.
Woodall, M. P., Hanley; Mr. J. Passmore Edwards,
honorable treasurer; Miss Florence Balgarnie, honorable secretary.

This has been further supplemented by the following list from the Philadelphia *Press* of Sunday, August
26, 1894, containing many English, and not a few names
of persons of great influence, natives of the United
States:—

Duke of Argyle, Sir John Gorst, member of Parlia-
ment for the University of Cambridge and student of
Social Phenomena; Justin McCarthy, Sir John Lub-
bock, Ellis Ashmead Bartlett, Rt. Rev. Ed. White
Benson, Archbishop of York and Primate of all England; Passmore Edwards, treasurer, who has in hand
5000 pounds to carry on the work of the committee;
Mrs. Humphrey Ward, president of the Women's
Auxilliary Branch of the League; Lady Henry Som-
erset, the Countess of Aberdeen; the Countess of
Meath, founder of the Ministering Children's League;
J. Keir Hardie. Americans—Richard Watson Gilder,
of Century Company; Samuel Gompers, labor leader;

Miss Frances Willard, Archbishop Ireland, Dr. John Hall, W. Bourke Cochran, Carl Schurz, Mgr. Ducey, Bishop David Lessums, of the Protestant Episcopal Diocese of Louisiana; Archbishop Francis Jansens, of the Roman Catholic Arch-Diocese of Louisiana; Bishop Hugh Miller Thompson, of Mississippi; Bishop A. Van de Vyer, of Virginia.

The Legislatures of Texas, Alabama and Florida have consented to give a hearing to deputations sent out by the League.

The following interesting and pathetic fact is stated (concerning the first contribution to the funds of the above-mentioned League) by Miss Wells in the Aug. 23d, 1894, issue of the New York *Age*:—

The first donation that the committee received came from a party of a dozen Africans who were in England. Desiring to show their appreciation of what had been done for me and the cause of the race, they sent 14 pounds, or nearly $70, as a testimonial of appreciation. I shall be glad to give a copy of their letter in another issue. We want the same voluntary response on this side to carry on the work here. Shall we have it?   IDA B. WELLS.

128 Clark street, Chicago, Ill.

Returning to the United States July 24, 1894, Miss Wells was enabled to be present in person at a meeting of endorsement of her work in England held at

Fleet Street A. M. E. Church, New York City. T. Thomas Fortune, editor of the New York *Age* and President of the National Afro-American League, had called for a national expression on Lynch Law by the various Leagues throughout the country, and the above-mentioned meeting voiced New York's Afro-American sentiment on the question.

The press comments on Miss Wells' work would already fill many volumes, some favorable, others unfavorable to the cause of the Afro-American, but all showing conclusively the truth of a statement made by Miss Wells in a recent issue of the *Age:*

"That the Afro-American has the ear of the civilized world for the first time since emancipation." Eminent Afro-American leaders, such as the Hon. Frederick Douglass; Rev. Harvey Johnson, D. D., Baltimore, Md.; Bishop H. M. Turner and Dr. H. T. Johnson, of the *Christian Recorder*, have endorsed Miss Wells' work, also the National Afro-American League, Equal Rights Council of Boston, Afro-American Leagues of Baltimore, Philadelphia, New Bedford, New Haven, Rochester, and other cities.

"CHICAGO, Aug. 18.—The Chicago Anti-Lynching Committee has effected permanent organization with the following officers: President, F. L. Barnett; vice-president, Mrs. J. C. Plummer; secretary, Dr. C. E. Bently; treasurer, C. H. Smiley. There is an executive committee of nine, two of whom are women. There is already a membership enrolment of 30 and the representative citizens of Chicago, including the pastors of the churches, have enlisted to fight Lynch Law.

" The Central Executive Council have organized at Brooklyn, N. Y., the following-named officers being elected: W. L. Hunter, president; Rev. A. J. Henry, vice-president; W. H. Dickerson, secretary; and Rev. W. T. Dixon, treasurer. Mr. S. R. Scottron, Rev. Lawton, Drs. W. A. Morton, Coffey and Harper and Rufus L. Perry are eminent workers in this cause."

Who shall say that such a work accomplished by one woman, exiled and maligned by that community among whom she had so long and so valiantly labored, bending every effort to the upbuilding of the manhood and womanhood of all races, shall not place her in the front rank of philanthropists, not only of the womanhood of this race, but among those laborers of all ages and all climes?

Before closing this chapter of race history, how shall we estimate those humble workers who have labored for the upbuilding of our churches and societies, the opening up everywhere to the race more favorable school privileges, such noble souls as Mary McFarland Jennings and Mrs. Mary Browne, wife of William Browne of The True Reformers; those dear ones who have so modestly ministered to the wants of the sick and afflicted until their record of good works has followed them abroad, as with Mrs. Florida Grant, the beloved wife of Bishop Abram Grant, and that sweet, quiet worker in the Master's Vineyard, Mrs. Eliza Turner, the deceased wife of Bishop H. M. Turner?

Two classes we have failed to mention thus far, but our hearts hold them in fullest remembrance: those uncrowned queens of the fireside who have been simply home-keepers, raising large families to a noble manhood and womanhood; among these stand forth pre-eminently Mrs. Elizabeth Steward, wife of Dr. T. G. Steward, and Mrs. Bishop B. T. Tanner, and those other sisters still dearer to us, whose work lies around us with its sweet fragrance until it seems almost too sacred to weave into this chaplet of pearls. Of this number are Martha Briggs, Rebecca Steward, Katie Campbell Becket, and Grace Douglass.

We close this tribute to Afro-American womanhood with a heart warmed and cheered, feeling that we have proved our case.

Hath not the bond-woman and her scarce emancipated daughter done what they could?

Will not our more favored sisters, convinced of our desires and aspirations because of these first few feeble efforts, stretch out the helping hand that we may rise to a nobler, purer womanhood?

A SKETCH OF AFRO-AMERICAN LITERATURE.

" THEY who have their eyes fixed in adoration upon the beauty of holiness are not far from the sight of all beauty. It is not permitted to us to doubt that in Music, in Painting, Architecture, Sculpture, Poetry, Prose, the highest art will be reached in some epoch of its growth by the robust and versatile race sprung from those practical idealists of the seventeenth century, those impassioned seekers after the invisible truth and beauty of goodness."—*Moses Coit Tyler.*

The intellectual history of a people or nation constitutes to a great degree the very heart of its life. To find this history, we search the fountain-head of its language, its customs, its religion, and its politics expressed by tongue or pen, its folklore and its songs. The history of the Afro-American race in this country may be divided into three epochs—the separation from native land and friends, and later arrival in this land of forced adoption. Next follows two hundred and fifty years of bondage and oppression mitigated only through the hope thrown upon life's pathway by the presence of hundreds of freemen of the race

(48)

eking out an existence hampered on all sides by caste prejudice. Later, an era of freedom covered by twenty years of emancipation, holding in name citizenship, but defrauded of its substance by every means that human ingenuity could devise. Again, the intellectual history of a race is always of value in determining the past and future of it. As a rule, a race writes its history in its laws and in its records. Not so the Afro-American: he could make no law; deprived of the opportunity to write, he could leave no written word; he could only protest against the injustice of his oppressors in his heart, in his song, and in his whispered consolations to the suffering and dying.

The heredity and evironment of a people fix their intellectual limitations as they do their moral and physical. Therefore, perhaps it would be said, these people can have no real literature; but in yet another sense let its successful achievement convince us of the accomplished fact. Every human attempt must have had its first, feeble, rudimentary steps, must have one day been the era of small things. The first tiny stream that at last swells to a broad river having therefore its own important place in the future life of that fact, so these faint, tottering intellectual steps must be worthy of record. With all its drawbacks the race has built up a literature of its own that must

4

be studied by the future historian of the life of the American nation. Afro-American literature in the United States, and by this we mean literature which has originated with the Afro-American, must be largely tinctured with the history of three great happenings in their lives. Torn from their home and kindred, they soon lost all memory of their native tongue, except as here and there some idiom survived. Their first faint gropings in the language of the new world were recitals of the woes they had suffered and the longing for home and loved ones. The soul felt desire to see again the land of their birth and look once more upon its beauty. But as memory of the fatherland became dimmed by time, the experiences of the life of bondage, its hardships and sufferings, its chastened joys and its future outlook toward the longed-for day of freedom that all believed would some day come, the ties of love and friendship formed, became the burden of their song.

At the time the slave trade started in this country, the possibilities of the new continent were new to the master; he had not become adjusted to his own novel environment. The newly imported Africans were largely descendants of the lowest type of African barbarism—history telling us they were mostly drawn from the coast tribes, who were easiest of capture, the white man fearing to go into the interior. The few belonging to the mountain tribes brought to this land were only such as had been held as prisoners of war by the coast tribes. The slaves were located in the warmest section of the New World, employed in the lowest forms of labor. Their environment was from every point of view hostile to intellectual development. They had been captured and enslaved that their toil might enrich another nation; they were reared in the midst of a civilization from whose benefits they were largely debarred; they were taught two things— reverence and obedience to authority as embodied in the master, and next in all of his race, and lastly to fear God. In spite of all impediments to intellectual advancement, here and there faint searchings after knowledge appeared among them. With a nature keenly alive to inquiry, the stories of the Bible took fast hold upon their imagination. The history of the children of Israel they made their own. As Moses through God became the deliverer of the Israelites, so would He give the oppressed ones of that day a deliverer. This seems to have been the first germ of intellectuality that appeared among them; this thought they wove into verse and sung and crooned as a lullaby. In their first attempts at literature may be found their origin—native Africans made Americans against their will—the tribes to which they belonged giving a clue to the differences in their powers of physical endurance or strength of character, when drawn from mountain or coastland. Their place of residence in their new home, largely a sojourner in the sunny South; their fear of the rigor of the northern and eastern climes; the troubles they had to contend with from within were those caused by the jealousy and suspicion implanted by their cunning masters, from without by the lack of opportunities for educational or spiritual growth, it being at that day against the law for an Afro-American to be found with a book, and a felony to teach one the alphabet. In the course of time, however, by stealth in the South and through the philanthropy of individuals of the North, largely members of the Society of Friends, they gained a foretaste of education. It has been said that oratory is the art of a free people, but this race even in the days of bondage and at the first faint breath of freedom, seem to have given birth to those who could rank with the masters of this art. The matchless oratory of Frederick Douglass, Samuel Ruggles Ward, Jabez Pitt Campbell and Joseph C. Price, has never been surpassed by men of any race on this continent. Scattered through every State in the Union, the Afro-American unconsciously imbibed the traits of character and order of thought of those among whom he dwelt. He became the Chesterfield of the South; his courtliness even in his master's cast-off belongings put that of the master to shame. The slave-mother's loving kindness to her own and her foster child became a proverb; her loving, wifely spirit of devotion and self-sacrifice dimmed the lustre of these virtues in her more favored sister of a fairer hue.

The preacher of this race has never been surpassed for his powers of imagery, his pathos, his abundant faith in the future states of reward and punishment. His faith in the word of God, even as a bondsman, made soft the dying pillow of many a passing soul; the quaintness and originality of his speech delighted many an auditor in the home circle, and his abounding love of great titles and high-sounding names has never ceased to amuse the student of this impressionable son of Ham.

The first written works of the Afro-American were not issued to make money, or even to create a literature of their own, but to form a liberal sentiment that would favor the abolition of slavery, or at least, the gradual emancipation of the slaves, and thus laboring they assisted the Anti-Slavery workers in the advancement of their cause. Thus, the speeches of Frederick Douglass, his "Life of Bondage," and other like writings were given to the world. At a later day, as opportunities for education advanced, and readers among their people increased, various weekly, annual, quarterly and monthly publications appeared. Here and there some more cultured and learned member of the race gathered into book-form scattered sermons, church history and poems. Within the past twenty years they have become, to a large extent, their own journalists, gathering and compiling facts about the race, forming plans to erect monuments to their heroes, recording the deeds of these heroes both in prose and verse. The despised Afro-American is learning daily to honor himself, to look with awe upon the future possibilities of his people within the life of this nation.

The first two books written by members of the race in America were by native Africans, who had for a time drifted to the shores of Europe, and there in that purer light of freedom published the outpourings of their burdened spirits, and at that early day, as at the present, the song was in the minor key, never rising to a glad and joyous note. Both books were well received, their merit recognized, and their authors honored with the love and confidence of those who had minds liberal enough to recognize the worth of a brother, although of sable hue. The first attempt at book-making by an Afro-American in the United States was, strange to say, from the pen of a woman, and was entitled " Poems on Various Subjects, Religious and Moral," by Phyllis Wheatley, servant to Mr. John Wheatley of Boston. The volume was dedicated to the Right Honorable the Countess of Huntington, by her much obliged, very humble and devoted servant, Phyllis Wheatley, Boston, June 12, 1773. A meekly worded preface occupies its usual place in this little book. Mr. Wheatley's letter of explanation of the difficulties encountered follows the preface. Fearing, as often occurred in those days of bitter race-hatred, that the authenticity of the poems would be questioned, an attestation was drawn up and signed by a number of worthy gentlemen.

Afro-Americans are born idealists; in them art, poetry, music, oratory, all lie sleeping. To these the first dawn of hope gave utterance. The little slave girl, in the safe, quiet harbor of her mistress' boudoir, takes heart of grace and tunes her lyre. Her verse shows the shadow of her unhappy lot, but rises above these sorrows and on the uplifted wings of song, floats to the starry heavens and consoles the afflicted, gives praise to the faithful ruler, breaks forth in love for the new home.

Phyllis Wheatley, from all accounts given of her from every source, was of a sweet, loving disposition, attaching herself readily to those with whom she came in contact by this especial trait in her character. Her book was written under the pleasantest auspices, surrounded by loving and appreciative friends, with a bright fire and friendly lamp in her room that she might get up at any moment and jot down the thought. The point is often discussed whether the poems of Phyllis Wheatley are of literary merit or simply curiosities as the work of an African child. That this gifted one died in her early womanhood would lead us to feel that longer life might have left to the world poems of greater strength and beauty. Yet, scan as often as we will or may the verses of Phyllis Wheatley, we claim for her the true poetic fire. In the poem to the Right Honorable the Earl of Dartmouth, the perfect rhythm, the graceful courtesy of thought, the burning love for freedom capture the heart. The "Farewell to America," the "Tribute to New England," have a sweetness and grace, a sprightliness and cheer all their own. Another proof of the genius of this young poetess may be found in the poem beginning, "Your Subjects Hope, Dread Sire." How these verses must have won the heart of His Most Excellent Majesty the King! what a flood of sympathy must have gone out to this young maiden in bondage, who could forget her sorrows in his joy!

A narrative by Gustavus Vassa, published October 2d, 1790, was the second volume written by an African made by force a resident of America. Prejudice being so great, this volume, as was Phyllis Wheatly's, was first published in England. The second edition was welcomed in his American home.

The writing of this little narrative, unlike the first, was accomplished under many hardships and difficulties, pursued by troubles and trials and dire calamities, yet it is a true and faithful account, written in a style that deserves respect. The following memorial to the English Parliament will give an idea of the style of the volume.

To the Lords spiritual and temporal, and the Commons of the Parliament of Great Britain.

My Lords and Gentlemen:—Permit me, with the greatest deference and respect, to lay at your feet this genuine narrative, the design of which is to excite in your august assemblies a sense of compassion for the miseries which the slave trade has entailed on my unfortunate country. I am sensible I ought to entreat your pardon for addressing to you a work so wholly devoid of literary merit, but as the production of an unlettered African who is actuated by the hope of becoming an instrument towards the relief of his suffering countrymen, I trust that such a man pleading in such a cause will be acquitted of boldness and presumption. May the God of Heaven inspire your hearts with peculiar benevolence on that important day when the question of abolition is to be discussed, when thousands in consequence of your decision are to look for happiness or misery.

I am, my Lords and Gentlemen,
Your most obedient and devoted humble servant,
GUSTAVUS VASSA.

"I believe it is difficult," writes Vassa, "for those who publish their memoirs to escape the imputation of vanity. It is, therefore, I confess, not a little hazardous in a private and obscure individual, and a stranger too, to thus solicit the indulgent attention of the public. If then the following narrative does not prove sufficiently interesting to engage general attention, let my motive be some excuse for its publication. I am not so foolishly vain as to expect from it either immortality or literary reputation. If it affords any satisfaction to my numerous friends, at whose request it has been written, or in the smallest degree promotes the interest of humanity, the end for which it was undertaken will be fully attained and every wish of my heart gratified. Let it therefore be remembered that in wishing to avoid censure, I do not aspire to praise." Says the Abbe Gregoire in his volume entitled "An Inquiry Concerning the Intellectual and Moral Faculties, or a Literature of Negroes:" "It is proven by the most respectable authority that Vassa is the author of this narrative, this precaution being necessary for a class of individuals who are always disposed to calumniate Negroes to extenuate the crime of oppressing them." Says the good Abbe in conclusion, "The individual is to be pitied who, after reading this narrative of Vassa's, does not feel for him sentiments of affection and esteem."

The second class of writers were natives of America, living in liberal communities, such as could be found in the New England and some of the Middle States. "Walker's Appeal" is one of the most notable of these volumes, as it counselled retaliation. The author's reward was a price upon his head. Writers, such as William Wells Brown, of "Rising Sun" fame; William C. Nell, with "Colored Patriots of the Revolution;" Frederick Douglass, Francis Ellen Watkins Harper, with other like workers, labored for the Anti-Slavery cause. Inspired with a hope of greater privileges for themselves and emancipation for their brethren in the South, they wrote with a burning zeal which had much to do with securing the end desired. After this came twenty-five years of freedom with its scores of volumes, such as Williams' "History of the Negro Race in America," Fortune's "Black and White," Bishop Gaines's "African Methodism in the South," Albery Whitman's "Poems," Crummel's "Greatness of Christ," Penn's "Afro-American Press," Scarborough's "Greek Grammar," Johnson's "Divine Logos," Bishop Payne's "History of African Methodism," Steward's "Genesis Reread."

This era produced history, narrative, fiction, biography, poetry and scientific works varying in grade of excellence, but yet all of invaluable interest; for in them is garnered that which must give inspiration to the youth of the race. Each had its effect of gaining the hearts of their enemy, winning respect and admiration, thus strengthening the bands of a common humanity. Simple and unadorned, these writings have a force and eloquence all their own that hold our hearts, gain our sympathies, fill us with admiration for the writers, for their persevering energy, their strong love of freedom, the impartiality of their reasoning. With what sincerity they bear testimony to the good they find even in their enemies. With what clear judgment they state the difficulties that surround their path. With what firm faith they look ever to the Ruler of all nations to guide this one to justice. Yes, this race is making history, making literature : he who would know the Afro-American of this present day must read the books written by this people to know what message they bear to the race and to the nation.

Of volumes of a later date all are more or less familiar. But we cannot forbear in closing to say a word of three recent race publications : " Iola, or The Shadows Uplifted," by Mrs. F. E. W. Harper, and "A Voice from the South, by a Black Woman of the South " (Mrs. A. J. Cooper). " Iola, or The Shadows Uplifted," is in Mrs. Harper's happiest vein. The scene is laid in the South, and carries us through the various stages of race history from slavery to this present

day.   All of the open and settled questions of the so-
called Negro problem are brought out in this little
volume.   In the opening and closing of many chap-
ters Mrs. Harper has risen to a height of eloquent
pleading for the right that must win for the race many
strong friends.   Mrs. A. J. Cooper has done for her
people a great service in collecting her various essays
into book form.   Together they make one of the
strongest pleas for the race and sex of the writer that
has ever appeared.   In this little volume she proves
that few of the race have sung because they could but
sing, but because they must teach a truth ; because of
the circumstances that environed them they have
always been, not primarily makers of literature, but
preachers of righteousness.

The third volume, "Aunt Lindy," by (Victoria
Earle) Mrs. W. E. Matthews, the last to appear, is a
beautiful little story and is deserving of careful study,
emanating as it does from the pen of a representative
of the race, and giving a vivid and truthful aspect of
one phase of Negro character.   It shows most conclusively the need of the race to produce its own
delineators of Negro life.

The scene is laid in Georgia.   A Cotton Exchange
has taken fire, the flames spreading to a neighboring
hotel, many of the inmates are wrapped in the flames
of the dread tyrant.   One, a silver-haired stranger, with

others is carried to neighboring homes for quiet and careful nursing.

"Good Dr. Brown" thinks of no other nurse so capable as "Aunt Lindy."

The old lady had been born in slavery, suffered all its woes, but in the joys of freedom had come to years of peace.

She welcomed the wounded sufferer, laid him in a clean, sweet bed that she had kept prepared hoping that some day one of her own lost children might return to occupy it.

As she stands by his side suddenly some feature, some word of the suffering one, brings back the past. Peering closely into the face of the restless sleeper she exclaims, "Great Gawd! it's Marse Jeems!"

Then begins the awful struggle in the mind of the poor freedwoman. The dreadful tortures of her life in bondage pass in review before memory's open portal. Shall vengence be hers? Shall she take from him the chance of life? Shall she have revenge, swift, sure and awful?

In these beautiful words Mrs. Matthews shows us the decision, how the loving forgiveness of the race, as it has always done, came out more than conqueror:

. . . .

"Soon from the portals of death she brought him, for untiringly she labored, unceasingly she prayed in her

poor broken way; nor was it in vain, for before the
frost fell the crisis passed, the light of reason beamed
upon the silver-haired stranger, and revealed in mystic
characters the service rendered by a former slave—
Aunt Lindy.

" He marvelled at the patient faithfulness of these
people.   He saw but the Gold—did not dream of the
dross burned away by the great Refiner's fire."

In this little story, and especially in its sequel, Mrs.
Matthews has given a strong refutation of the charges
made against the race by Maurice Thompson in his
" Voodoo Prophecy," where he makes the poet of wild
Africa to say:

" A black and terrible memory masters me,
   The shadow and substance of deep wrong.
   .   .   .   .

I hate you, and I live to nurse my hate,
   Remembering when you plied the slaver's trade
In my dear land. . . . . How patiently I wait
          The day,
          Not far away,
  When all your pride shall shrivel up and fade !
   .   .   .   .

As you have done by me so will I do
   By all the generations of your race."

Only the race itself knows its own depth of love, its powers of forgiveness. In the heart of this race, if the American nation will only see it so, they have the truest type on earth of forgiveness as taught by the Redeemer of the world.

This blood-bought treasure, bought with a Saviour's love, a nation's dreadful agony, is yet spurned and trampled on by professed followers of the meek and lowly Jesus.

As we remember that the one novel written in America that captured the hearts of the world sung the wrongs of this people ; that the only true American music has grown out of its sorrows ; that these notes as sung by them melted two continents to tears ; shall we not prophesy of this race that has so striven, for whom John Brown has died, with whom one of Massachusetts' noblest sons felt it high honor to lie down in martial glory, to whom a Livingstone bequeathed to their ancestors in the dark continent that heart that in life beat so truly for them ? Shall we not prophesy for them a future that is commensurate with the faith that is in them ?

LIST OF AFRO-AMERICAN PUBLICATIONS.

Phyllis Wheatley's Poems, 1773.
Narrative, by Ouladal Ecquino or Gustavus Vassa.
Walker's Appeal.
Light and Truth, Lewis, Boston, 1844.
Whitfield's Poems, 1846.
Martin Delaney's Origin of Races.

My Bondage and Freedom, Frederick Douglass, 1852.
Autobiography of a Fugitive Negro, 1855.
Twenty Years a Slave, Northrup, 1859.
Rising Son and Black Man, William Wells Brown.
William C. Nell. Colored Patriots of the Revolution.
Tanner's Apology for African Methodism.
Still's Underground Railroad.
Colored Cadet at West Point, Flipper.
Music and Some Highly Musical People.
My Recollections of African Methodism, Bishop Wayman.
First Lessons in Greek, Scarborough.
Birds of Aristophanes, Scarborough.
History of the Black Brigade, Peter H. Clark.
Higher Grade Colored Society of Philadelphia.
Uncle Tom's Story of His Life, by Henson.
Greatness of Christ. Black Woman of the South.
Future of Africa, Alexander Crunnell, D. D.
Not a Man, and Yet a Man, Albery Whitman.
Mixed Races, J. P. Sansom.
Recollections of Seventy Years, Bishop D. A. Payne, D. D.
Memoirs of Rebecca Steward, by T. G. Steward.
In Memoriam.
Catherine S. Beckett, Rev. L. J. Coppin.
A Brand Plucked from the Fire, Mrs. Julia A. J. Foote.
Thoughts in Verse, George C. Rowe.
Cyclopædia of African Methodism, Bishop Wayman.
Night of Affliction and Morning of Recovery, J. H. Magee.
The Negro of the American Rebellion, William Wells Brown.
African Methodism in the South, or Twenty-five Years of Freedom,
    Bishop Wesley J. Gaines.
Men of Mark, Wm. J. Simmons, D. D.
Afro-American Press, I. Garland Penn.
Lynch Law, Iola. (Ida B. Wells.)
Women of Distinction, L. A. Scruggs, M. D.
Genesis Reread; Death, Hades and the Resurrection, T. G. Stew-
    ard, D. D.
Corinne, Mrs. Harvey Johnson.
A Voice from the South, by a Black Woman of the South, Mrs. A. J.
    Cooper.
Two volumes written by whites, yet containing personal writings by
    the Negro Race.
A Tribute to the Negro.

5

An Inquiry Concerning the Moral and Intellectual Faculties, or a Literature of the Negroes, by Abbe Gregoire.
The Cushite, Dr. Rufus L. Perry.
Noted Negro Women, Majors.
"Aunt Lindy," Victoria Earle.
Tuskegee Lectures, Bishop B. T. T. Tanner, D. D.
The Rise and Progress of the Kingdoms of Light and Darkness, or the Reigns of the Kings Alpha and Abaden, by Lorenzo D. Blackson.
History of the Negro Race in America, Geo. Williams.
History of the A. M. E. Z. Church.
History of the First Presbyterian Church, Gloucester.
History of St. Thomas' Protestant Episcopal Church, Wm. Douglass.
History of the A. M. E. Church, D. A. Payne.
Black and White, T. Thomas Fortune.
Liberia, T. McCants Stewart.
Bond and Free, Howard.
Poems, Novel Iola, Mrs. F. E. W. Harper.
Morning Glories (Poems), Mrs. Josephine Heard.
Negro Melodies, Rev. Marshall Taylor, D. D.
The New South, D. A. Straker.
Life of John Jasper, by himself.
Church Polity, Bishop H. M. Turner.
Digest of Theology, Rev. J. C. Embry, D. D.
Sense and Method of Teaching, W. A. Williams.
Brother Ben, Mrs. Lucretia Coleman.
The Divine Logos, H. T. Johnson, D. D.
The Relation of Baptized Children to the Church, L. J. Coppin, D. D.
Domestic Education and Poems, D. A. Payne.
The Negro in the Christian Pulpit, Bishop J. W. Hood.

We should be glad if authors would send us the names of omitted volumes to be used in a possible future edition.

THE AFRO-AMERICAN WOMAN IN VERSE.

EVERY age and clime has been blessed with sweet singers, both in song and verse. Many women have attained to rare excellence in each of these lofty vocations. Among modern songsters Jenny Lind, Patti and Parepa have won golden laurels. In verse Elizabeth Barrett Browning stands pre-eminent. She not only honored her own English island home, but sunny Italy, the land of her adoption, has been purified and sweetened by the power of her verse. And with rare appreciation and devotion has this land of poetry and art showered honors on this sweet singer.

That we, too, of the African race have equally shared in the gift of the muses, having had sweet singers born among us, I have chosen for my theme, " The Afro-American Woman in Verse."

Have we not had among us Elizabeth Greenfield, "The Black Swan," and have we not now Madame Selika, Flora Batson, Madame Jones and Madame Nellie Brown Mitchell? Crowned heads, as well as the uncrowned populace, have delighted to do honor to many of the sweet singers of our race. And have not two continents hung in breathless silence on the melody floating heavenward from the lips of our Jubilee Singers?

That we have also among us those with rare talent for verse we hope to prove in the limits of this short article.

During the year 1761 there sailed from Africa for America a slave ship. Among its passengers was a little girl, then seven or eight years of age. The following is from Williams' "History of the Negro Race:" "She was taken, with others, to the Boston slave market. There her modest demeanor and intelligent countenance attracted the attention of Mrs. John Wheatley, who purchased her. It was her intention to instruct the child in ordinary domestic duties, but she afterward changed her mind and gave her careful training in book knowledge. The aptness of the child was a surprise to all who came in contact with her. In sixteen months from her arrival she had learned the English language so perfectly as to be able to read the most difficult portions of Scripture with ease, and within four years she was able to correspond intelligently. She soon learned to read and even translate from the Latin. One of Ovid's tales was her first attempt. It was published in Boston and England and called forth much praise. Pious, sensitive and affectionate by nature, Phyllis soon became endeared not only to the family to whom she belonged, but to a

large circle of friends.   Mrs. Wheatley was a benevolent woman, and took great care of Phyllis, both of
her health and education.   Emancipated at the age
of twenty, she was taken to Europe by a son of Mrs.
Wheatley." . . . "She was heartily welcomed by
the leaders of society of the British metropolis, and
treated with great consideration.   Under all the trying
circumstances of social life among the nobility and
rarest literary genius of London, this redeemed
child of the desert coupled to a beautiful modesty
the extraordinary powers of an incomparable conver-
sationalist.   She carried London by storm.   Thought-
ful people praised her, titled people dined her, and
the press extolled the name of Phyllis Wheatley, the
African poetess. . . . In 1773 she gave a volume
of poems to the world.   It was published in London.
It was dedicated to the Countess of Huntington, with
a picture of the poetess and a letter of recommendation, signed by the Governor and Lieutenant-Governor
of Boston.   In 1776 she addressed a poem to George
Washington, which pleased the old warrior very much.
Unfortunately no copy of this poem can be found at the
present date."   In a letter, however, he wrote to Joseph
Reed, bearing date of the 10th of February, 1776,
from Cambridge, Washington refers to it.   He says:
" I recollect nothing else worth giving you the trouble
of, unless you can be amused by reading a letter and

poem addressed to me by Miss Phyllis Wheatley. In searching over a parcel of papers the other day, in order to destroy such as were useless, I brought it to light again. At first, with a view of doing justice to her poetical genius, I had a great mind to publish the poem; but not knowing whether it might not be considered rather as a mark of my own vanity than a compliment to her, I laid it aside till I came across it again in the manner just mentioned."

This gives the world an "inside" view of the brave old general's opinion of the poem and poetess; but the outside view, as expressed by Washington himself to Miss Phyllis, is worthy of reproduction at this point.

CAMBRIDGE, 28 February, 1776.

MISS PHILLIS:—Your favor of the 26th of October did not reach my hands till the middle of December. Time enough you will say to have given an answer ere this. Granted. But a variety of important occurrences, continually interposing to distract the mind and withdraw the attention, I hope will apologize for the delay, and plead my excuse for the seeming but not real neglect. I thank you most sincerely for your polite notice of me in the elegant lines you enclosed; and however undeserving I may be of such encomium and panegyric, the style and manner exhibit a striking proof of your poetical talents; in honor of which, and as a tribute justly due to you, I would have published the poem had I not been apprehensive that, while I only meant to give the world this new instance of your genius, I might have incurred the imputation of vanity. This, and nothing else, determined me not to give it place in the public prints.

If you should ever come to Cambridge, or near headquarters, I shall be happy to see a person so favored by the muses, and to whom nature has been so liberal and beneficent in her dispensations.

I am, with great respect, your obedient, humble servant,
GEORGE WASHINGTON.

We regret our loss of this poem on account of the great general's modesty, but rejoice in the fact that the greater number of Miss Wheatley's poems were published in one volume, and given to the world.

We will quote as largely as the limits of this paper will allow from this volume.

A FAREWELL TO AMERICA.

Adieu New England's smiling meads,
    Adieu the flowery plain ;
I leave thine opening charms, O spring,
    To tempt the roaring main.

.   .   .   .

For thee, Britannia, I resign
    New England's smiling fields,
To view again her charms divine,
    What joy the prospect yields !

The love of freedom is beautifully expressed in a poem " To the Right Honorable William Earl of

Dartmouth, His Majesty's Principal Secretary of State for North America."

Hail, happy day, when, smiling like the morn,
Fair Freedom rose New England to adorn :
The northern clime beneath her genial ray,
Dartmouth, congratulates thy blissful sway.
Elate with hope her race no longer mourns,
Each soul expands, each grateful bosom burns.

.   .   .   .

No more America in mournful strain
Of wrongs and grievance unredressed complain.

.   .   .   .

Should you, my Lord, while you pursue my song,
Wonder from whence my love of Freedom sprung,
Whence flow these wishes for the common good,
By feeling hearts best understood,
I, young in life, by seeming cruel fate,
Was snatched from Afric's fancied happy seat :
What pangs excruciating must molest,
What sorrow labor in my parents' breast ?
Steel'd was the soul and by no misery mov'd
That from a father seized his babe beloved:
Such, such my case.   And can I then but pray
Others may never feel tyrannic sway ?

We cannot refrain from giving one more proof of
the intelligence and genius of this young African
poetess.   It is dedicated to " The King's Most Excellent Majesty," on the repeal of the Stamp Act.

Your subjects hope, dread Sire,
The crown upon your brows may flourish long,
And that your arm may in your God be strong.
O may your sceptre num'rous nations sway,
And all with love and readiness obey!

.   .   .   .

But how shall we the British King reward!
Rule thou in peace, our father and our lord!
Midst the remembrance of thy favors past,
The meanest peasant most admires the last—
May George, belov'd by all the nations round,
Live with the choicest constant blessings crowned!

At the death of Mrs. John Wheatley, Phyllis married
John Peters, a grocer of Boston, of whom it is said,
"he wore a wig, carried a cane, and quite acted out
the 'gentleman.'" But not being a gentleman, except
in seeming, he soon grew jealous of the attention his
wife received, and by his abuse and harsh treatment
shortened her life, her death occurring December
5th, 1784, in the thirty-first year of her life. She was
the mother of one child.

Esteemed by all and beloved by many, her influence
upon the rapidly growing Anti-Slavery sentiment was
considerable. Her works were pointed to as an unan-
swerable argument in favor of the humanity of the
Negro and his capability to receive culture.

From 1784 until 1890, there has not been a volume of poems written by a colored woman pub-

lished in America. Several pamphlets and scattered poems have appeared from time to time in magazines and papers either devoted to the interest of the race or edited by colored men. But the race has never failed through all these long years of bondage to embalm in song and verse the beautiful thoughts that years of ceaseless oppression could not entirely banish from their minds. Through all the long years of slavery, through all the aftermath of the reconstruction era, the weird, plaintive melodies that welled up in their souls passed down from mother to child, and at last bore fruit when sung by the band of singers from the South land, the sweet-voiced Jubilee Singers, who sung a University * into existence.

During the time of the publication of the Liberator, by William Lloyd Garrison, and at the time of the Anti-Slavery movement in Philadelphia, Sarah Forten, a woman of large culture and great refinement, wrote several poems. Some of these were published by Mr. Garrison in the Liberator. We present our readers the following:

THE GRAVE OF THE SLAVE.

The cold storms of winter shall chill him no more,
His woes and his sorrows, his pains are all o'er;
The sod of the valley now covers his form,
He is safe in his last home, he feels not the storm.

---

* Fisk University, Tenn.

The poor slave is laid all unheeded and lone,
Where the rich and the poor find a permanent home;
Not his master can rouse him with voice of command;
He knows not and hears not his cruel demand;

Not a tear, nor a sigh to embalm his cold tomb,
No friend to lament him, no child to bemoan;
Not a stone marks the place where he peacefully lies,
The earth for the pillow, his curtain the skies.

Poor slave, shall we sorrow that death was thy friend,
The last and the kindest that heaven could send?
The grave of the weary is welcomed and blest;
And death to the captive is freedom and rest.

ON THE ABANDONMENT OF PREJUDICE.

We are thy sisters; God has truly said
That of one blood the nations he has made.
O Christian woman, in a Christian land,
Canst thou unblushing read this great command?

Suffer the wrongs which wring our inmost heart
To draw one throb of pity on thy part!
Our skins may differ, but from thee we claim
A sister's privilege and a sister's name.

The "Grave of the Slave" became quite popular, and
was set to music by Frank Johnson, the great negro
musician of Philadelphia.

The next woman we shall delight to honor is Mrs.
Frances Ellen Watkins Harper. Mrs. Harper has

been an Anti-Slavery lecturer in the days now past,
and wrote several poems of great worth in that movement.   Since the emancipation of the slaves she has
been a lecturer in the temperance cause, and is now
Superintendent in the National Woman's Temperance
Union, and is also a director in the Woman's Congress, of which she has been one of the ablest members.

Both as a writer of prose and poetry Mrs. Harper's
talents are too well known to need eulogy at our hands.
She is still among us, laboring with her pen, as her
poem, entitled " The Dying Bondsman," and her contribution to the symposium on the Democratic return
to power, both published in the *A. M. E. Church Review*, attest.   She likewise contributed to the "Alumni
Magazine " and many of the first-class weeklies published by our race.

We give a brief quotation from her beautiful poem,
entitled " Moses.   A story of the Nile."

THE DEATH OF MOSES.—CHAPTER IX.

His work was done ; his blessing lay
Like precious ointment on his people's head,
And God's great peace was resting on his soul.
His life had been a lengthened sacrifice,
A thing of deep devotion to his race,
Since first he turned his eyes on Egypt's gild

And glow, and clasped their fortunes in his hand
And held them with a firm and constant grasp.
But now his work was done; his charge was laid
In Joshua's hand, and men of younger blood
Were destined to possess the land and pass
Through Jordan to the other side.

While the Anti-Slavery movement was in progress
in Massachusetts, Miss Charlotte Forten, of Philadelphia, now Mrs. Francis Grimke, of Washington, D. C.,
wrote several articles on Southern life. These found
ready acceptance at the hands of the publishers of the
"Atlantic Monthly." Miss Forten wrote often, both
in prose and verse, but many very beautiful poems
were never published. As the wife of Dr. Grimke she
has been so occupied with work more directly confined to the church and locality, that nothing from her
pen has appeared for some years. We have been
honored, however, with a few lines from private collections of herself and friends.

CHARLES SUMNER.

(*On seeing some pictures of the interior of his house.*)

Only the casket left! The jewel gone,
Whose noble presence filled these stately halls,
And made this spot a shrine, where pilgrims came—
Stranger and friend—to bend in reverence

Before the great pure soul that knew no guile;
To listen to the wise and gracious words
That fell from lips whose rare, exquisite smile
Gave tender beauty to the grand, grave face.
Upon these pictured walls we see thy peers—
Poet, and saint, and sage, painter and king,—
A glorious band; they shine upon us still;
Still gleam in marble the enchanting forms
Whereon thy artist eye delighted dwelt;
Thy favorite Psyche droops her matchless face,
Listening, methinks, for the beloved voice
Which nevermore on earth shall sound her praise.
All these remain—the beautiful, the brave,
The gifted silent ones,—but thou art gone !
Fair is the world that smiles upon us now;
Blue are the skies of June, balmy the air
That soothes with touches soft the weary brow.

Mrs. M. E. Lambert scarce needs an introduction to
the readers of the *Review*. The beautiful " Hymn to
the New Year " is still singing its sweet message to
us. The following triumphant strains are from her
Easter hymn, as published in " St. Matthew's Journal,"
of which she is editor.

CHRIST IS RISEN.

*Now is Christ risen from the dead, and become the first
fruits of them that slept.*—I Cor. xv. 20.

The Lord is risen ! In the early dawn
  Nature awakens to the glad surprise,

And incense sweet from blossoming vale and lawn
   Fills the fair earth, and circles to the skies.

    .   .   .   .   .   .

O, Death, where thy terrors, thy darkness and
       gloom!
  And where, evermore, is thy victory, O grave!
Behold, the Great Conqueror illumines the tomb,
   Where shall rest the redeemed He hath
      suffered to save.
O'er sin hath He triumphed, o'er ruler and foe,
   O'er scorn and rude insult, o'er mockery and shame;
Whose pain and whose anguish we never can know,
   But whose love through it all remaineth the same.

    .   .   .   .   .   .

Alleluia! He is risen, the song has begun,
   Alleluia! Let the music reach each echoing shore,
He is risen! He is risen! the theme of every tongue,
   To whom be endless glory, both now and evermore.

Miss Cordelia Ray, one of the teachers of New
York City, has won for herself a place in the front
rank of our literary workers. A poem, entitled
"Dante," contributed to a late issue of the *Review*, received well deserved praise, and many readers hope
we shall again be charmed with offerings from the
same pen. We regret our inability to quote sufficiently from poems sent us to do justice to the author's
talent, but space forbids.

COMPENSATION.

Men who dare mighty deeds with dauntless will,
    Oft meet defeat,—not glorious victory;
But the uplifting souls to undreamed heights,
    May not of poorest laurels worthy be.

There is a heroism born of pain,
    Whose recompense in noble impulse lies;
And sometimes tears that e'en from grief did flow
    Are changed to joy-drops in pathetic eyes.

From out the din of mighty orchestras,
    The sweetest, purest tones are oft evolved;
So, from the discord of our restless lives,
    May come sweet harmony when all is solved.

SUNSET PICTURE.

The Sun-god was reclining on a couch of rosy shells,
And in the foamy waters Nereids tinkled silver bells,
That lent the soft air sweetness, like an echoed seraph-
        song,
Floating with snow-flake hush the aisles of Paradise
        along.

The Sun-god wove bright flowers, gold and purple in
        their hue,
And to the smiling Nereids tenderly the blossoms
        threw;
The sapphire seas were shadowy, like an eye with
        dreamy thought,
Where all the soul's mute rapture—a prisoned star—
        is caught.

The billows' rainbow splendor, like a strange enchant-
　　　ing dream,
In fading, softened slowly to a trembling pearly
　　　gleam ;
And soon the wondrous Sun-god, and the Nereids
　　　and the sea
Had vanished ; one gray-tinted cloud alone remained
　　　for me.

IN MEMORIAM.

A leaf from Freedom's golden chapter fair,
We bring to thee, dear father !　Near her shrine
None came with holier purpose, nor was thine
Alone the soul's mute sanction ; every prayer
Thy captive brother uttered found a share
In thy wide sympathy ; to every sign
That told the bondman's need thou didst incline,
No thought of guerdon hadst thou but to bear
A loving part in Freedom's strife.　To see
Sad lives illumined, fetters rent in twain,
Tears dried in eyes that wept for length of days—
Ah ! was not that a recompense for thee ?
And now, where all life's mystery is plain,
Divine approval is thy sweetest praise.

This beautiful verse appears in the opening pages of
an exquisite memorial volume to the memory of
Charles B. Ray, prepared by his loving daughters,
Florence and H. Cordelia Ray, of New York City.

　Mrs. Mary Ashe Lee, a graduate of Wilberforce
6

University and wife of Bishop B. F. Lee, has, by her
intelligence and sympathy, done much to inspire
the students of that University with a love for broad
culture, true refinement and high moral aims.   Mrs.
Lee has frequently added to the grace of public oc-
casions at the college by her contributions of verse.
One of the most beautiful, "Tawawa," commemorates
the former Indian name of the present site of Wilberforce.   We give a short extract:

> Where the hoary-headed winter
> Dwells among the leafless branches,
> Filling all the earth with whiteness,
> Freezing all the streams and brooklets,
> And with magic fingers working
> With his frosty threads of lace work
> Wraps the land in sweet enchantment.

> .   .   .   .   .   .

> Thus the site of Wilberforce is,
> Wilberforce, the colored Athens.
> But another name she beareth,
> Which the Indians call Tawawa.
> I will tell you of Tawawa;
> She the pride in all of Piqua,
> Pride of all the Shawnee nation,
> Child of love and admiration.
> In the bosom of the forest,
> Of Ohio's primal forest,

Stood a wigwam, lone and dreary,
With its inmates sick and weary ;
Snow-drifts covered all the doorway ;
Still the snow kept falling, falling,
And the winds were calling, calling
Round the wigwam of Winona.
Far had gone the good Owego
To the lakes in north Ohio,
Looking for some ven'son for her :
Scarce was everything that winter.
Thus Winona, weeping, sighing,
On her bed of deerskin lying,
Pressing fondly to her bosom,
With a mother's love, a blossom,
Which the Spirit sent to cheer her,
Sent to coo and nestle near her ;
Cried Winona, in her anguish,
For she feared the child would languish,
"Oh, sweet Spirit, hear thy daughter ;
Give us bread, as well as water !"
Then a vision passed before her,
And its scenes did quite restore her,
For she saw the dogwood blossom.
Now she had her father's wisdom,
So she knew that these white flowers
Came to speak of brighter hours,
Speak of sunshine and of plenty.
"Ah, my wee, wee pickaninny,
I will call you the *white flower*,
My Tawawa, whitest flower !"

Another poem by Mrs. Lee, entitled " Afmerica,"

and of a more recent date, contains many beautiful
thoughts expressed in a most chaste and exquisite
style.

AFMERICA.

Hang up the harp! I hear them say,
Nor sing again an Afric lay,
The time has passed; we would forget—
And sadly now do we regret
There still remains a single trace
Of that dark shadow of disgrace,
Which tarnished long a race's fame
Until she blushed at her own name;
And now she stands unbound and free,
In that full light of liberty.
"Sing not her past!" cries out a host,
"Nor of her future stand and boast.
Oblivion be her aimed-for goal,
In which to cleanse her ethnic soul,
And coming out a creature new,
On life's arena stand in view."
But stand with no identity?
All robbed of personality?
Perhaps, this is the nobler way
To teach that wished-for brighter day.
Yet shall the good which she has done
Be silenced all and never sung?
And shall she have no inspirations
To elevate her expectations?
From singing I cannot refrain.
Please pardon this my humble strain.

With cheeks as soft as roses are,
And yet as brown as chestnuts dark,
And eyes that bo   ow from a star
A tranquil yet a brilliant spark ;
Or face of olive with a glow
Of carmine on the lip and cheek,
The hair in wavelets falling low,
With jet or hazel eyes that speak ;
Or brow of pure Caucasian hue,
With auburn or with flaxen hair
And eyes that beam in liquid blue—
A perfect type of Saxon fair.
Behold this strange, this well-known maid,
Of every hue, of every shade !

        .   .   .   .   .

Oh ye, her brothers, husbands, friends,
Be brave, be true, be pure and strong ;
For on your manly strength depends
Her firm security from wrong.
O ! let your strong right arm be bold,
And don that lovely courtesy,
Which marked the chevaliers of old.
Buttress her home with love and care,
Secure her those amenities
Which make a woman's life most dear.
Give her your warmest sympathies,
Thus high her aspirations raise
For nobler deeds in coming days.

A beautifully bound volume of poems has recently
appeared under the authorship of Mrs. Josephine

Heard.   The charm of the fair author's personality runs through these verses full of poetic feeling, bright and sparkling.   And yet the closing verse holds our memory longest, and in our own humble judgment is the gem of the collection.

AN EPITAPH.

When I am gone,
Above me raise no lofty stone
Perfect in human handicraft,
No upward pointing, gleaming shaft.
Say this of me, and I shall be content,
That in the Master's work my life was spent;
Say not that I was either great or good,
But, Mary like, she hath done what she could.

From time to time there have appeared within the columns of the A. M. E. Review, Christian Recorder, Ringwoods' Journal, The Monthly Review, New York Age, Our Women and Children, and Howard's Magazine, poems of exquisite beauty.   From these we quote, here and there, a gem serene.

APRIL.

BY JOSEPHINE B. C. JACKSON.

Robes of bright blue around her form are swaying,
And in her bosom dewy violets lie;
While the warm sun rays on her girdle playing,
Give it the rainbow's soft and varied dye.

Over the meadow where the grass is growing,
She sprinkles early flowers of every hue;
Weeping, she strews them, and the bright tears
    flowing,
Bathe every leaflet with a shining dew.

With stately step, and crowned with crimson roses
She comes; and sighing, April bows her head;
Then May the white lids on the sweet eyes closes,
And lays fair April with her flowers—dead.
Jacksonville, Ill.

FLEETING YEARS.

Swiftly beyond recall,
    The years are fleeting fast;
The brittle threads of time,
    Will gently break at last.
O man of wisdom, canst thou tell,
Why human hearts love here to dwell?

Is it because earth yields
    So many treasures rare?
Is it because life gives
    So many pleasures fair?
Cease, doubting soul; it may be fate
That bids thee through the years to wait.

Bright flowers and pricking thorns
    Bestrew this life's highway,
Where weary feet still tread
    The changing paths of day.
But there is bliss for all the tears
That seem to dim the fleeting years.

We know, beyond the veil,
    There is some hidden joy;
'Tis worth this life to live,
    That we may then employ
Our trembling lips, in praise sublime,
Beyond the boundless space of time.

And shall we then despise
    The day of smallest things?
Ah, no! these souls of ours
    Shall soon on angel's wings
Be borne aloft, when years shall cease,
To rest in perfect joy and peace.

                              FRANCIS A. PARKER.
Hamilton, Bermuda.

AT BAY ST. LOUIS.

BY MISS ALICE RUTH MOORE.

Soft breezes blow, and swiftly show,
Through fragrant orange branches parted,
A maiden fair, with sun-flecked hair
Caressed by arrows, golden darted.
The vine-clad tree holds forth to me
A promise sweet of purple blooms,
A chirping bird, scarce seen, but heard,
Sings dreamily, and sweetly croons,
                    At Bay St. Louis.

The hammock swinging, idly singing, lissome, nut-
                brown maid
Swings gaily, freely, to and fro.

The curling, green-white waters, casting cool, clear
           shade,
Rock small, shell boats that go
In circles wide, or tug at anchor's strain,
As though to skim the sea with cargo vain,
         At Bay St. Louis.

The maid swings slower, slower to and fro,
And sunbeams kiss gray, dreamy half-closed eyes;
Fond lover creeping on with footsteps slow,
Gives gentle kiss, and smiles at sweet surprise.

     .   .   .   .

The lengthening shadows tell that eve is nigh,
And fragrant zephyrs cool and calmer grow,
Yet still the lover lingers, and scarce-breathed sigh
Bids the swift hours to pause, nor go,
         At Bay St. Louis.

THOUGHTS ON RETIRING.

BY LUCY HUGHES BROWN, M. D.

Oh Lord, the work thou gavest me
    With this day's rising sun,
Through faith and earnest trust in Thee,
    My Master, it is done.

And ere I lay me down to rest,
    To sleep—perchance for aye—
I'd bring to thee at Thy request
    A record of the day.

And while I bring it willingly
And lay it at Thy feet,
I know, oh, Saviour, certainly,
That it is not complete.

Unless Thy power and grace divine,
Upon what I have wrought,
Shall in its glorious fulness shine,
Oh Lord, the work is naught.

A RETROSPECT.

BY L. H. BROWN, M. D.

Oh God, my soul would fly away
Were it not fettered by this clay;
I long to be with Thee at rest,
To lean in love upon Thy breast.

Here in this howling wilderness,
With enemies to curse, not bless,
I feel the need of Thy strong hand
To guide me to that better land.

How oft, oh God, I feel the sting
Of those whose evil tongues would wring
The heart of any trusting one
As did the Jews to Thy dear Son.

Yet in this hour of grief and pain,
Let me not curse and rail again;
But meek in prayer, Lord, let me go
And say, " They know not what they do."

Lord, when this hard-fought battle's o'er,
And I shall feel these stings no more,
Then let this blood-washed spirit sing
Hosannah to my Lord and King.

GOD'S CHILDREN—THE FATHERLESS.

BY IDA F. JOHNSON.

Speak softly to the fatherless,
  And check the harsh reply
That sends the crimson to the cheek,
  The teardrop to the eye.
They have the weight of loneliness
  In this rude world to bear;
Then gently raise the falling bud,
  The drooping floweret spare.

Speak kindly to the fatherless—
  The lowliest of their band
God keepeth as the waters
  In the hollow of his hand.
'Tis sad to see life's evening sun
  Go down in sorrow's shroud;
But sadder still when morning's dawn
  Is darkened by a cloud.

Look mildly on the fatherless;
  Ye may have power to wile
Their hearts from sadden'd memory
  By the magic of a smile.

Deal gently with the little ones ;
    Be pitiful, and He,
The Friend and Father of us all,
    Shall gently deal with thee.

A REST BEYOND.

BY MISS KATIE D. CHAPMAN.

If this world were all, and no
Glorious thought of a Divine
Hereafter did comfort me, then
Life with too much pain were
        Fraught and misery.
I should not care to live another
Day, with burdened heart and naught
To cheer my soul upon its lonely way,
        From year to year.
So many cares beset me on my way ;
So many griefs confront me in the
Road, how wretched I, no hope,
No faith to-day, in Heaven
        and God.
The friends I love, for whom my life
Is spent, do oft misjudge and rob
Me of their love.   Ah, if I had
No hope in Jesus, sent down from above !
Why should I care to stay in such
A race ? far rather give the
Bitter struggle o'er and die,
Caring not to face what the
        Future hath in store.

> But just beyond is Heaven's
> Eternal shore, a mansion
> Waiteth for each sincere soul,
> A blessed rest forever more
> Is at the goal.

Of the history of these sweet singers we know but little. Of Miss Jackson, Miss Johnson, and Miss Chapman, naught but their song. Mrs. Frances A. Parker, we learn, purposes bringing out a pamphlet of her collected writings, bearing the title, " Woman's Noble Work."

Mrs. Lucy Hughes Brown, the author of the two sweet poems, " Thoughts on Retiring " and " A Retrospect," is a graduate from Scotia Seminary, N. C.; later as the wife of Rev. David Brown, of the Presbyterian church, Wilmington, N. C., she was enabled to do much philanthropical work for her race. Mrs. Brown received the degree of M. D. from the Women's Medical College, Philadelphia, March, '94.

Miss Alice Ruth Moore, through a complimentary editorial in the *Woman's Era*, we learn, is a Southerner by birth, and we feel that the *Era* has voiced our own sentiments in so cordially thanking the editor of the *Monthly Review* for introducing to us this charming writer.

During the year 1859, there was published in New York City, that Mecca of authors and editors, *The*

Anglo-African, a magazine of merit. Its editor was Thomas Hamilton. An able corps assisted him in the work; among them was Charles Ray, George B. Vashon, James McCune Smith, and other well-known literary men. From this magazine we have culled the two closing poems of this paper. They rank well with the writers of this present generation. Mrs. Harper was then in her youth. Grace Mapps belonged to a family noted for its acquirements in music, literature and art. Her aunt, Mrs. Grace Douglass, wrote a most beautiful tract that was published in the history of the First African Presbyterian Church, of Philadelphia. Her cousin, Sarah M. Douglass, taught for over fifty years most successfully the preparatory department of the Philadelphia Institute for Colored Youth. Miss Mapps, also, for several years, taught as a member of the faculty of the same institution, now presided over so ably by Mrs. Fanny J. Coppin, wife of Dr. Levi Coppin, of the A. M. E. Church.

GONE TO GOD.

MRS. F. E. W. HARPER.

Finished now the weary throbbing,
Of a bosom calmed to rest;
Laid aside the heavy sorrows,
That for years upon it prest.

All the thirst for pure affection,
All the hunger of the heart,
All the vain and tearful cryings,
All forever now depart.

Clasp the pale and faded fingers,
O'er the cold and lifeless form;
They shall never shrink and shiver,
Homeless in the dark and storm.

Press the death-weights calmly, gently,
O'er the eyelids in their sleep;
Tears shall never tremble from them,
They shall never wake to weep.

Close the silent lips together,
Lips once parted with a sigh;
Through their sealèd moveless portals,
Ne'er shall float a bitter cry.

Bring no bright and blooming flowers,
Let no mournful tears be shed,
Funeral flowers, tears of sorrow,
They are for the cherished dead.

She has been a lonely wanderer,
Drifting on the world's highway;
Grasping with her woman's nature
Feeble reeds to be her stay.

God is witness to the anguish
Of a heart that's all alone;

Floating blindly on life's current,
Only bound unto His throne.

But o'er such Death's solemn angel
Broodeth with a sheltering wing;
Till the helpless hands, grown weary,
Cease around earth's toys to cling.

Then kind hands will clasp them gently,
On the still and aching breast;
Softly treading by they'll whisper
Of the lone one gone to rest.

LINES.

BY GRACE A. MAPPS.

Oh harvest sun, serenely shining
    On waving fields and leafy bowers,
On garden wall and latticed vine
    Thrown brightly as in by-gone hours;
Oh ye sweet voices of the wind,
    Wooing our tears, in angel tones;
Friends of my youth, shall I not weep?
    Ye are still here, but *they* are gone.

I see the maples, tossing ever
    Their silvery leaves up to the sky;
Still chasing o'er the old homestead's walls
    The trembling light, their shadows fly.
Familiar forms and gentle faces
    Once glanced beneath each waving bough,
And glad tones rung: shall I not weep
    That all is lone and silent now?

Nay, for like heavenly whispers stealing,
   Comes now this memory divine,
Where thy clear beams, Oh sun of autumn,
   Through the stained windows richly shine;
A solemn strain, the organ blending,
   Like a priest's voice, its glorious chord,
Is on the charmed air ascending;
   " Come, let us sing unto the Lord."

And while the earth, year after year,
   Puts all her golden glory on,
And like it, God's most holy love
   Comes now, with every morning's dawn,
" Singing unto the Lord," I love,
   With all the hosts that speak His praise.
I may not walk the earth alone,
   Nor sorrow for departed days.

I know the friends I loved so well,
   Through the years of their life-long race,
Lifted sweet eyes of faith to God,
   And now they see His blessed face.
Thou, Lord, forever be my song,
   And I'll not weep for days gone by;
But give Thee back each hallowed hour,
   A seed of immortality.

Here and there, from this garden of poesy, we have
culled a blossom; but how many gardens of beauty
have we not looked upon ?   And yet, we must close.
knowing " the half hath not been told."

7

OUR WOMEN IN JOURNALISM.

THE heredity and environment of women has for
many ages circumscribed them to a certain routine
both of work and play. In this century, sometimes
called the "Nineteenth Century," but often the
"Women's Century," there has been a yielding of the
barriers that surround her life. In the school, the
church, the state, her value as a co-operative is being
widely discussed. The co-education of the sexes,
the higher education of woman, has given to her life a
strong impetus in the line of literary effort. Perhaps
this can be more strongly felt in the profession of
journalism than in any other. On every hand journals published by women and for women are multiply-
ing. The corps of lady writers employed on most of
our popular magazines and papers is quite as large as
the male contingent and often more popular if not as
scholarly. We can realize what this generation would
have lost if the cry of "blue stocking" had checked
the ambition of our present women writers. The
women of our race have become vitalized by the
strong literary current that surrounds them. The

number is daily increasing of those who write com-
mendably readable articles for various journals published by the race. There was a day when an Afro-
American woman of the greatest refinement and culture
could aspire no higher than the dressmaker's art, or later
who would rise higher in the scale could be a teacher,
and there the top round of higher employment was
reached. But we have fallen on brighter days, we
retain largely the old employments and have added to
this literary work and its special line of journalistic
effort.

New lines are being marked out by us ; notice
"Aunt Lindy" and "Dr. Sevier" in the *Review*. The
success of this line of effort is assured and we hail it
with joy. Our women have a great work to do in
this generation ; the ones who walked before us could
not do it, they had no education. The ones who
come after us will expect to walk in pleasant paths of
our marking out. Journalism offers many inducements,
it gives to a great extent work at home ; sex and race
are no bar, often they need not be known ; literary
work never employs all one's time, for we cannot write
as we would wash dishes. Again, our quickness of per-
ception, tact, intuition, help to guide us to the popular
taste ; her ingenuity, the enthusiasm woman has for all
she attempts, are in her favor. Again, we have come on
the world of action in a century replete with mechan-

ical means for increasing efficiency ; woman suffrage is about to dawn.   Our men are too much hampered by their contentions with their white brothers to afford to stop and fight their black sisters, so we slip in and glide along quietly   We are out of the thick of the fight. Lookers-on in Venice, we have time to think over our thoughts, and carry out our purposes ; we have everything to encourage us in this line of effort, and so far I have found nothing to discourage an earnest worker. All who will do good work can get a hearing in our best Afro-American journals.   In the large cities especially of the North we have here and there found openings on white journals.   More will come as more are prepared to fill them and when it will have become no novelty to be dreaded by editor or fellow-reporters. To women starting in literary work I would say, Write upon the subjects that lie nearest your heart; by that means you will be most likely to convince others.   Be original in title, conception and plan.   Read and study continuously.   Study the style of articles, of journals.   Discuss methods with those who are able to give advice.   Every branch of life-work is now being divided into special lines and the literary field shares in the plan marked out by other lines of work ; so much is this the case that the name of Cable, or Tourgee, or Haygood, suggests at once southern Negro life; Edward Atkinsson, food; Prof. Shaler, scientific research, and so on ad infinitum. Our literati would do well to follow the same plan ; it may have its disadvantages, but it certainly has also its advantages. To those who aspire to become journalists we only give the old rule, enter the office, begin at the lowest round and try to learn each department of work well. Be thankful for suggestions and criticism, make friends, choose if possible your editor, your paper, be loyal to both, work for the interest of both. See that your own paper gets the best, the latest news. If a new idea comes to you, even if it is out of your line of work, talk over it with him. Study papers, from the design at the top, the headings, the advertisements, up to the editorials. Have an intelligent comprehension of every department of work on the paper. As a reporter I believe a lady has the advantage of the masculine reporter in many respects. She can gain more readily as an interviewer access to both sexes. Women know best how to deal with women and the inborn chivalry of a gentleman leads him to grant her request when a man might have been repulsed without compunction. In seven years' experience as an interviewer on two white papers I have never met with a refusal from either sex or race. If at first for some reason they declined, eventually I gained my point. Another pleasant feature of this as of all other employment is its comradeship; one can always find a helper in a fellow-worker. I have received some such kind, helpful letters; one from Mrs. Marion McBride, President of the New England Women's Press Association comes to my mind; another from Mrs. Henry Highland Garnet of N. Y. Here and there pleasant tokens of esteem and co-operation greet me. I have been thanked heartily in many strange places, by many new and unaccustomed voices, for helpful words spoken in the long ago. To the women of my race, the daughters of an an oppressed people, I say a bright future awaits you. Let us each try to be a lamp in the pathway of the co-laborer a guide to the footsteps of the generation that must follow. Let us make, if we can, the rough places smooth; let us write naught that need cause a blush to rise to our cheek even in old age. Let us feel the magnitude of the work, its vast possibilities for good or ill. Let us strive ever not to be famous, but to be wisely helpful, leaders and guides for those who look eagerly for the daily or weekly feast that we set before them.

Doing this, our reward must surely come. And when at some future day we shall desire to start a women's journal, by our women, for our women, we will have built up for ourselves a bulwark of strength; we will be able to lead well because we have learned to follow. May these few words, allied to the bright and shining examples of such women as Mrs.

Frances Ellen Watkins Harper, Mrs. Fanny Jackson Coppin, Mrs. Sara M. Douglass, and other consistent, industrious workers, serve as a stimulus to some one who is strong of will, but weak of purpose, or to another whose aspiration is to become a journalist, but who fears to launch her little bark on the waves of its tempestuous sea.

OUR AFRO-AMERICAN REPRESENTATIVES AT THE WORLD'S FAIR.

It was the earnest wish of the Afro-Americans that they should be given representation upon the National Committee of the World's Fair; in this they were sadly disappointed. A fair representation, however, was accorded them upon the State Boards.

The first appointment was made by Governor Robert E. Pattison, of Pennsylvania.

To Robert Purvis, of Philadelphia, was accorded the honor of being made a Commissioner for the State of Pennsylvania. Mr. Purvis is well past the threescore years and ten usually allotted to mortals of to-day. The death of the poet Whittier leaves him the only surviving member of the body of sixty persons that signed the Declaration of Sentiments of the National Committee, which met in Philadelphia fifty-nine years ago to found the American Anti-Slavery Society. The life-work of Robert Purvis has been the amelioration of the condition of the weaker race, to which he is allied by perhaps one-eighth a strain of blood.

Left in comfortable circumstances by a wealthy father, with a brilliant education and large native talent, he has devoted his life to fighting the battles of Afro-Americans. Mr. Purvis has a face that even with advanced years is yet strikingly strong and beautiful; tall and commanding in stature, with most courtly manners, his presence adds grace and distinction to any body of which he is a member. His home life is like that of a refined and cultured member of the Society of Friends; his present wife indeed being one of that sect.

An intelligent family of children surround him in his old age, all being the offspring of his first wife, formerly a Miss Forten, of Philadelphia. One son, Dr. Charles Purvis, was for a number of years Surgeon-in-Chief of the Freedmen's Hospital, at Washington, D. C.

Mr. Purvis' home is full of books, pictures and curios relative to the history of the race. The University of Pennsylvania has dedicated an alcove to Anti-Slavery literature in its new library building, the alcove being named the Purvis Alcove. Mr. Purvis and Dr. Furness have given to the library many valuable works, among them a complete edition of Wm. Lloyd Garrison's Liberator. Within these later years this venerable philanthropist has largely confined his labors to securing opportunities for intelligent members of the race in higher grades of work.

The most valued possession of this great survivor

of the Anti-Slavery days, is a painting of Cinque, the
hero of the L'Amistead, painted by the artist, Jocelyn.
Cinque, being an African captive thrust into slavery,
captured the vessel and put the crew in irons, carried
the vessel to England, and thus, through international
law, secured his freedom. The Pennsylvania Historical
Society, and the New Haven Historical Society, have
both expressed a desire to become possessors of this
valuable historical painting.

.   .   .   .

"A Woman's Auxilliary Committee to represent the
work of women through the State of Pennsylvania, was
formed to work with the State Board. One of the first
ladies appointed on this board, was Miss Florence A.
Lewis, of Philadelphia. It can truly be said that Miss
Lewis represents in her personality the symmetrical
development and complete womanhood that it is possible for the Afro-American woman to attain under
favoring circumstances.

"Born and raised in Philadelphia, she is one of that
younger group of women who have made the most of
the opportunities of a wide-awake northern city. Miss
Lewis was graduated from the Institution for Colored
Youth, and passed successfully the State examination
for certificate to teach in the public schools. She
taught in one of the Grammar schools for a number of
years, at the same time doing literary work for several

papers. In course of time Miss Lewis found that she could profitably devote all her time to literature, and for the last five years she has been connected with the Philadelphia *Press* in the weekly edition, of which she conducts a department, besides contributing special work to the other editions. Miss Lewis is also connected with the magazine *Golden Days*, and writes over various signatures for newspapers and magazines in several cities. She is also one of the Advisory Board of the Citizens' National League, of which Judge Tourgee is the founder and President.

"Bright, witty and interesting, Miss Lewis has a charm and refinement of manner that make her a worthy addition to Pennsylvania's 'Group of Noble Dames.'

.   .   .   .

"The position on the Board of Woman Managers of the State of New York for the Columbian Exposition was entirely unsought by Miss Imogene Howard. Her experience has been a very pleasant one thus far. Her special position on the board is as one of five of the 'Committee on Education.'

"Joan Imogene Howard was born in the city of Boston, Mass. Her father, Edward F. Howard, is an old and well-known citizen of that city, and her mother, Joan L. Howard, now deceased, was a native of New York. She has one sister, Miss Adeline T.

Howard, the principal of the Wormley School, Washington, D. C., and one brother, E. C. Howard, M. D., a prominent physician in the city of Philadelphia.

" Having a mother cultured, refined and intellectual, her earliest training was received from one well qualified to guide and direct an unfolding mind. At the age of fourteen, having completed the course prescribed in the Wells' Grammar School, Blossom street, Boston, she graduated with her class, and was one of the ten honor pupils who received silver medals.

" Her parents encouraged her desire to pursue a higher course of instruction, and consequently after a successful entrance examination, she became a student at the ' Girls' High and Normal School.' She was the first colored young lady to enter and, after a three years' course, to graduate from this, which was, at that time, the highest institution of learning in her native city.

" A situation as an assistant teacher in Colored Grammar School No. 4—now Grammar School No. 81—was immediately offered. Here she has labored ever since endeavoring to harmoniously develop the pupils of both sexes who have been committed to her care.

" Many of her pupils have become men and women of worth, and hold positions of honor and trust.

" For several years an evening school, which was

largely attended, and of which she was principal, was carried on in the same building.

" As time advances more is required of all individuals in all branches of labor. Teaching is no exception, and in recognition of this she took a course in 'Methods of Instruction" at the Saturday sessions of the Normal College, of N. Y. She holds a diploma from this institution [1877], and thus has the privilege of signing 'Master of Arts' to her name. This year [1892] still another step has been taken, for, after a three years' course at the University of the City of New York, she has completed the junior course in Educational History, Psychology, Educational Classics and Methodology. As a result of this she has had conferred upon her the degree of Master of Pedagogy."

.   .   .   .   .   .

" Nothing but pleasant surprises await the people of America in getting acquainted with the ever increasing number of bright Afro-American men and women whose varied accomplishments and achievements furnish some of the most interesting episodes in newspaper literature.

"Some months ago wide publicity was given to the brilliant sallies of wit and eloquence of a young Afro-American woman of Chicago in appealing to the Board of Control of the World's Columbian Exposition in behalf of the American Negro. The grave and matter-of-fact members of the Commission were at first inclined to treat lightly any proposition to recognize the Afro-American's claim to representation in the World's Fair management. They soon found, however, that puzzling cross-questions and evasions awakened in this young woman such resources of repartee, readiness of knowledge and nimbleness of logic that they were amazed into admiration and with eager unanimity embraced her arguments in a resolution of approval, and strongly recommended her appointment to some representative position. The name of this bright lady is Mrs. Fannie Barrier Williams, and a closer knowledge of herself and history reveals the interesting fact that there is something more to her than ability to speak brilliantly. She was born in Brockport, N. Y., where her parents, Mrs. and the late A. J. Barrier, have been highly esteemed residents for nearly fifty years. Mrs. Williams is *petite* in size, and her face is one of rare sweetness of expression. In the pure idyllic surroundings of her home, in the quiet and refined village of Brockport, she had the very best school advantages.

" She was graduated from the college department of the State Normal School very young and began at once to teach school. For about ten years she was a successful teacher in the public schools of Washington, D. C., and resigned only when she became the wife of her present husband, Mr. S. Laing Williams, a well educated and ambitious young lawyer of the Chicago bar. Mrs. Williams early evidenced a decided talent for drawing and painting. While teaching in Washington she diligently exhausted every opportunity to develop her artistic instincts. She became a student in the studios of several Washington artists and further studied to some extent in the New England Conservatory and private studios of Boston. Her cleverest work has been that of portraits. At the New Orleans Exposition some years ago her pieces on exhibition were the theme of many favorable criticisms by visiting artists. In conversation Mrs. Williams is delightfnlly vivacious and pungent, and displays an easy familiarity with the best things in our language.

"With no cares of children she lives an active life. She is secretary of the Art Department of the Woman's Branch of the Congress Auxiliaries of the World's Columbian Exposition. This Committee has the active and honorary membership of the most distinguished women artists of the world, and Mrs. Williams enjoys the esteem of all who know her in this highly important branch of the World's Fair.

"She is also an active member of the 'Illinois Woman's Alliance,' in which she serves as chairman of the Committee on 'State Schools for Dependent Children.' She is likewise actively interested in the splendid work of the Provident Hospital and Training School, perhaps the most unique organization for self-helpfulness ever undertaken by the colored people of the country.

"Mrs. Williams' home life is unusually charming and happy. The choice of pictures and an ample library give an air of refinement and culture to her pretty home. She and her husband are active members of All Souls' Unitarian Church, of Chicago, and the Prudence Crandall Study Club. Mrs. Williams manifests an intelligent interest in all things that pertain to the well-being of the Afro-Americans and never hesitates to speak or write when her services are solicited. Her wide and favorable acquaintance with nearly all the leading Afro-American men and women of the country, and her peculiar faculty to reach and interest influential men and women of the dominant race in presenting the peculiar needs of her people, together with her active intelligence, are destined to make Mrs. Williams a woman of conspicuous usefulness."

.   .   .   .   .   .

Next to that of Mr. Robert Purvis, the most important appointment made in connection with the race at the World's Fair is that of Hon. Hale G. Parker, Commissioner at Large. Mr. Parker is a citizen of St. Louis, Mo., but a native of Ripley, Ohio; he is

a son of John Percival Parker, proprietor and manager of the Phœnix Foundry and Machine Works,
the largest on the Ohio river between Cincinnati and
Portsmouth. Mr. Hale is a graduate of Oberlin College, class of '73. He entered upon the field of educational work after graduation, but a few years later determined upon the profession of law as his life-work.
Graduating from the St. Louis Law School in '82, he
was a few months later admitted to the bar. In connection with the duties of his professional life, he has had
charge of the introduction of the J. P. Parker patents
in the South and West. Mr. Parker has proven one
of the most energetic workers on the World's Fair
Commission. He sat for the first time with the
National Commission in September and voted for
the $5,000,000 loan.

Mr. J. E. Johnson, of Baltimore, held for several
months a position as assistant upon the Government
Board. Mrs. A. W. Curtis, of Chicago, held for a
short time the position of " Secretary of Colored
Interests of the World's Fair."

The last appointment was that of Mrs. S. L. Williams, New Orleans, to the Educational Committee of
the State Board for the World's Fair. Mrs. Williams is
the originator, president, secretary, and treasurer of
an orphan asylum for girls. The institution was
opened August 24, 1892, with the enrolment of 69

orphans. The organization in its one year of existence has gathered a membership of 700, and received for support $1,755. Two entertainments are
given yearly for its maintenance. The life of this
noble woman is being given to the uplifting of the
girlhood of the race that needs, perhaps, more than
any other in all this fair land, the guidance and fostering care of such a noble, Christian motherhood.

THE OPPOSITE POINT OF VIEW.

HOME is undoubtedly the cornerstone of our beloved Republic. Deep planted in the heart of civilized humanity is the desire for a resting place that may be called by this name, around which may cluster life-long memories. Each member of a family after a place is secured, helps to contribute to the formation of the real and ideal home. Men's and women's desires concerning what shall constitute a home differ largely, sex counting for much, past environment for more. Man desires a place of rest from the cares and vexations of life, where peace and love shall abide, where he shall be greeted by the face of one willing to conform to his wishes and provide for his comfort and convenience—where little ones shall sweeten the struggle for existence and make the future full of bright dreams.

Woman desires to carry into effect the hopes that have grown with her growth, and strengthened with her strength from childhood days until maturity; love has made the path of life blend easily with the task that duty has marked out. Women picture their material home from its outer walls to the last graceful interior decoration thousands of times before it becomes an accomplished fact. In imagination the children of their love have twined their arms around their necks, dropped kisses upon their lips and filled their ears with the most loving name of mother. In this home of her dreams she has reigned queen of hearts, dispensing joy and peace to the dear ones who have placed their hearts in her keeping. Marriage constitutes the basis for the home; preceding this comes courtship; preceding it, should have been, and we believe has been, a degree of love. It is largely the fashion of the world to laugh at first love, to give it in derision the appellation of calf or puppy love, but to a mother the knowledge that the warmest affection of her child's heart is passing into the keeping of another (it may be for weal or it may be for woe) can never be a subject for mirth. Love is a reality; its influence may make life most worth living, or blast for time and eternity. Let us look at it as a mother must, as an entrance upon the Holy of Holies. The prevalent opinion concerning courtship is, that it is an era of deception.

We differ from the accepted opinion. Remembering the environment that surrounds every courtship we must admit that it lends itself readily to deception, but that the parties interested desire to deceive we greatly doubt. The girl and her lover are each placed under the pleasantest circumstances; relieved of all care, going where they like, seeing the one they admire most, dressed in apparel that becomes them well, pleasing and desiring to be pleased, what wonder if both act more kindly to each other at such a time and under such auspices than they do towards the world that surrounds them, opposing perhaps their every desire. When I was a girl teaching a school in the suburbs of Philadelphia, one unlettered but close masculine observer used to say of the men who stood in the above position, "Yes, they're lying, of course; but lying goes with courting." Another more refined feminine observer used to say earnestly, but with a sigh, "Honey, courting is mighty pretty business; but courting is no more like marrying than chalk is like cheese." Possibly all my experienced readers will admit that courting *is mighty pretty business*, especially the making-up process that is so often gone through, and also think there was a grain of truth in the other sage observations. And yet, to a certain extent, both were wrong; it is simply that circumstances alter cases.

Let us believe that the young people do not intend to deceive, but that being happy, it is easy to try to make others happy. Simply having turned to the looking-glass of another's face a smiling countenance, they have been met with a smile. At the close of a successful courtship, comes marriage, the basis of which may be real love, or ambition in its various guises. Many wonder that so many people separate, my wonder is that so many remain together. Born in different places, reared differently, with different religious and political opinions, differing in temperament, in educational views, at every point, what wonder strife ensues. But we will consider in this paper the life of those who elect to remain together whether life is a flowery path or overgrown with briers and thorns. Now, first, here I must explain that I am about to look at the opposite side of a much discussed question. The pendulum will swing in this paper in the opposite direction to the one generally taken.

The conservatives can take the median line with the pendulum at a standstill if they so desire. For several years, every paper or magazine that has fallen into our hands gave some such teaching as this: "The wife must always meet her husband with a smile." She must continue in the present and future married life to do a host of things for his comfort and convenience; the sure fate awaiting her failure to follow this advice being the loss of the husband's affection and the mortification of seeing it transferred to the keeping of a rival. She must stay at home, keep the house clean, prepare food properly and care for her children, or he will frequent the saloon, go out at night and spend his time unwisely at the least. These articles may be written by men or by women, but the

moral is invariably pointed for the benefit of women;
one rarely appearing by either sex for the benefit of
men. This fact must certainly lead both men and
women to suppose that women need this teaching
most; now I differ from this view of the subject. In
a life of some length and of close observation, having
been since womanhood a part of professional life, both
in teaching, preaching and otherwise, where one re-
ceives the confidences of others, I have come to the
conclusion that women need these teachings least.

I have seen the inside workings of many homes; I
know there are many slatterns, many gossips and poor
cooks; many who are untrue to marital vows; but on
the whole, according to their means, their opportunities
for remaining at home, the irritating circumstances
that surround them (and of our women especially),
tempted by two races, they do well. After due
deliberation and advisedly I repeat that they (remembering the past dreadful environment of slavery) do well.
Man as often as woman gives the keynote to the home-
life for the day; whether it shall be one of peace or strife.
The wife may fill the house with sweet singing, have the
children dressed and ready to give a joyful greeting
to the father; the breakfast might be fit to tempt an
epicure, and yet the whole be greeted surlily by one
who considers wife and home but his rightful convenience. I may not be orthodox, but I venture to

assert that keeping a clean house will not keep a man at home; to be sure it will not drive him out, but neither will it keep him in to a very large extent. And you, dear tender-hearted little darlings, that are being taught daily that it will, might as well know the truth now and not be crying your eyes out later.

Dear Willie can go out at night, yes, a little while even every night, and not be going to the bad nor failing to do his duty. Now let me tell you an open secret and look about you where you live and see if I am not right. The men that usually stay in at night are domestic in their nature, care little for the welfare or approval of the world at large, are not ambitious, are satisfied with being loved, care nothing for being honored. The men who used when single to kiss the babies, pet the cat, and fail to kick the dog where they visited are the men who remain at home most when married. A man who aspires to social pre-eminence, who is ambitious or who acquires the reputation of being a man of judgment and knowledge, useful as a public man, will be often out at night even against his own desires, on legitimate business. By becoming a member of many organizations it may become necessary for him to spend most of his evenings out, sacrificing his own will to the will of the many. Again, men after working at daily drudgery come home to their families, eat the evening meal, hear the day's doings,

read the paper and then desire to meet with some
masculine friends to discuss the topics of the day.
The club, the church, the street corner or a chum's
business place may be the meeting place. Bad men
go out for evil purposes; to be sure, many men, social
by nature, are tempted by the allurements of the
saloon and the chance of meeting their boon compan-
ions. But these men would do the same if they had
no home, or whether it was clean or not. Wives
should be kind, keep house beautifully, dress beautifully
if they can; but after all this is accomplished their husbands will be away from home possibly quite as much
for the above-given reasons. Women must not be
blamed because they are not equal to the self-sacrifice
of always meeting husbands with a smile, nor the wife
blamed that she does not dress after marriage as she
dressed before; child-birth and nursing, the care of
the sick through sleepless, nightly vigils, the exactions
and irritations incident to a life whose duties are made
up of trifles and interruptions, and whose work of
head and heart never ceases, make it an impossibility
to put behind them at all times all cares and smile
with burdened heart and weary feet and brain.

Small means, constant sacrifice for children prevent
the replenishment of a fast dwindling wardrobe. Husbands and fathers usually buy what they *need* at least
most mothers and wives will not even do that while

children need anything. The great inducement for a woman to fulfil these commands is that she may retain her husband's love and not forfeit her place to a rival. Suppose some one should tell a man, " Now you must smile at your wife always, in her presence never appear grumpy, dress her in the latest style, and so on, or else she will transfer her affections to the keeping of another." What would be his reply? We all know. And yet women need love to live and be happy, are supposed to be most susceptible to love and flattery, and men therefore ought to fear this fate most, and the daily record teaches the fact if the magazine writers fail to do so. A good husband will do his duty even if the wife fails, as so many wives are doing to-day with bad husbands. The man who wants to lead a reckless life, will complain of his wife's bad housekeeping, extravagance, the children's noise or, if not blessed with offspring, still complains that this fact makes home less interesting; but let me tell you, friend, it is all an excuse in nine cases out of ten. A husband's ill-doing is never taken as an excuse for a wife's turning bad, and why should a man be excused for doing wrong, if he has a bad wife? If he be the stronger-minded one, especially. If a husband is a true one in any sense of the word, his transference of the kiss at the door from the wife to the firstborn that runs before her to greet him will not cause even a sigh of regret.

Doing the best she can in all things will be appreciated by a true husband.   The one remaining thought unmentioned is *temper*, the disposition to scold and nag.   Now no man desires a scolding, nagging wife, and no child desires such a mother; but saints are rare and I don't believe that history past or present proves that saintly women have in the past or do now *gain men's love oftenest or hold it longest.*   The two women, one white, another colored, that I sorrowed with over recreant husbands, were true, loving wives; one had just saved her small earnings toward buying the husband a birthday present and had unsuspectingly kissed good-bye the partner of his flight.   The other clasped more lovingly the hand of the baby boy that most resembled him and only spoke of the facts as occasion required it in business concerning the property he had left behind; both men had found no fault with these wives, treated them kindly up to the last hour when they deserted them forever.   Neither sugar nor pickles would be a good diet, but most of us could eat a greater quantity of pepper hash than of sugar after all.   I believe that a woman who has a mind and will of her own will become monotonous to a less extent than one so continuously sweet and self-effacing; and I believe history proves it.

It may be humanity or masculinity's total depravity, but I believe more men tire of sweet women than even of scolds, and yet I do not desire to encourage the growth of this obnoxious creature. The desirable partner for a successful, peaceful married life is a woman of well-balanced temperament, who is known among her associates as one not given to what is often called fits of temper, and yet withal possessing a mind of her own. Perhaps my thought is best expressed in this extract from " Whimsicalities of Women " by Mrs. Frank Leslie in the *Sunday Press:*

" Women's nerves are lightly set; the jar that sets them all in a thrill passes unfelt over the heavier organization of a man ; the breeze that to him is only a pleasant stimulus is to her a devastating storm. For here is a truth which I present to the consideration of my sister women, and I assure them that it is the fruit of much observation and study of mankind. A woman's little tempers will in the course of years make an impression upon a man's estimate of her that no after time can undo; while, if she once truly love him, years of bickering or even ill-treatment on his part are wiped away and forgotten by the caresses of his returning love, or by the faltering farewell of his dying breath.

"A woman's resentment of the little offences offered her by the man she loves is like the sand upon the beach, so lightly ruffled, so easily heaved into chasms and mountains, but so sure to be placated by the turn

(Midori)

Digital collection →

History Makers
black
newspaper

?

Evelyn Cunningham

●

Raking

I like to rake the lea...

motion wit...

Into a great big hun...

leav...

of the tide, so easily restored to the full integrity of its original condition. But the man's consciousness of injuries is like the rock lying so stolidly upon that shifting beach. The winds blow the sand across him, but it soon blows off again. The waves dash over, and seem to leave no mark, but the years go by, and twice every day the sand and the waves together grind away a little and a little of the substance of the rock, and after many years, if the sand says, ' I am tired of this useless warfare, let us be as we were at first,' the rock must sadly answer, ' Nay, that cannot be, for the years have worn away what no years can restore. We can only make the best of what is left.' "

It is not possessing a temper, but continuous out-bursts of ill-temper that undermine true happiness. The home should be founded on right principles, on mor-ality, Christian living, a due regard to heredity and envi-ronment that promise good for the future. With these taken into consideration, backed by love, or even true regard, with each having an abiding sense of duty and a desire to carry out its principles, no marriage so contracted can ever prove a failure.

A LOFTY STUDY.

In these days of universal scribbling, when almost every one writes for fame or money, many people who are not reaping large pecuniary profits from their work do not feel justified in making any outlay to gratify the necessities of their labors in literature.

Every one engaged in literary work, even if but to a limited extent, feels greatly the need of a quiet nook to write in. Each portion of the home seems to have its clearly defined use, that will prevent their achieving the desired result. A few weeks ago, in the course of my travels, I came across an excellent idea carried into practical operation, that had accomplished the much-desired result of a quiet spot for literary work, without the disarrangement of a single portion of the household economy. In calling at the house of a member of the Society of Friends, I was ushered first into the main library on the first floor. Not finding in it the article sought, the owner invited me to walk upstairs to an upper library. I continued my ascent until we reached the attic. This had been utilized in such a way that it formed a comfortable and acceptable study. I made a mental note of my surroundings. The room was a large sloping attic chamber. It contained two windows, one opening on a roof; another faced the door: a skylight had been cut directly overhead, in the middle of the room. Around the ceiling on the side that was not sloping ran a line of tiny closets with glass doors. Another side had open shelves. On the sloping side, drawers rose from the floor a convenient distance. The remaining corner had a desk built in the wall; it was large and substantial, containing many drawers. Two small portable tables were close at hand near the centre.

An easy chair, an old-fashioned sofa with a large square cushion for a pillow, completed the furniture of this unassuming study. Neatness, order, comfort reigned supreme. Not a sound from the busy street reached us. It was so quiet, so peaceful, the air was so fresh and pure, it seemed like living in a new atmosphere.

I just sat down and wondered why I had never thought of this very room for a study. Almost every family has an unused attic, dark, sloping, given up to odds and ends. Now let it be papered with a creamy paper, with narrow stripes, giving the impression of height; a crimson velvety border. Paint the woodwork a darker shade of yellow, hang a buff and crimson portière at the door. Put in an open grate; next widen the windowsills, and place on them boxes

of flowering plants. Get an easy chair, a desk that suits
your height, and place by its side a revolving book-
case, with the books most used in it. Let an adjustable
lamp stand by its side, and with a nice old-fashioned
sofa, well supplied with cushions, you will have a study
that a queen might envy you. Bright, airy, cheerful,
and almost noiseless, not easy of access to those who
would come only to disturb, and far enough away to
be cosy and inviting, conferring a certain privilege on
the invited guest.

These suggestions can be improved upon, but the
one central idea, a place to one's self without disturbing
the household economy, would be gained.

Even when there is a library in the home, it is used
by the whole family, and if the husband is literary in
his tastes, he often desires to occupy it exclusively at
the very time you have leisure, perhaps. Men are so
often educated to work alone that even sympathetic
companionship annoys. Very selfish, we say, but we
often find it so—and therefore the necessity of a study
of one's own.

If even this odd room cannot be utilized for your
purposes, have at least your own corner in some
cheerful room. A friend who edits a special department in a *weekly* has in her own chamber a desk with
plenty of drawers and small separate compartments.
The desk just fits in an alcove of the room, with a re-

volving-chair in front. What a satisfaction to put everything in order, turn the key, and feel that all is safe—
no busy hands, no stray breeze can carry away or disarrange some choice idea kept for the future delectation of the public! Besides this, one who writes
much generally finds that she can write best at some
certain spot. Ideas come more rapidly, sentences
take more lucid forms. Very often the least change
from that position will break up the train of thought.

CASTE IN INSTITUTIONS DEVOTED TO THE EDUCATION OF THE COLORED RACE.

By the educational statistics of the last census there were 124 institutions for the instruction of the colored race, having an enrolment of 15,404 students, requiring 576 instructors.

The greater number of institutions devoted exclusively to Negro education are situated in the South. The larger portion of the work has been and still is carried on by denominational enterprise. Possibly the most important part of the work has been under the supervision of the American Missionary Association, the Presbyterian Board of Missions for Freedmen, and the Freedmen's Aid Society of the Methodist Episcopal Church.

It is a *well known fact* that a few of these institutions employ colored men in their Faculties; and we have endeavored to secure information as to the *actual percentage* of colored persons serving as Professors in institutions, but have failed to receive a reply to our queries.

Although a number of these institutions have been

in existence from 20 to 30 years, this absence is notice-
able. Unlike other educational institutions, the preference (where it is possible) is not given to their own
alumni. At the time of the founding of these institutions
the colored race had within its bounds few men of superior education; but with the aid of such institutions,
and the opening of the doors of all the higher grade
colleges of the North, East, and West, the reverse
has now become true and large numbers of colored men
and women are now thoroughly competent for such
positions.

The *continued failure* of these institutions to acknowledge this fact, to employ any considerable number of colored men in the Faculties, and to seek the
patronage of colored men of wealth and culture as
advisers on the Board of Trustees, has led the colored
alumni, and many friends of education, to feel that
there is a *deep-seated cause* for this neglect of colored
graduates; and that the explanation lies in caste
prejudice. This charge, when made by the colored
men, is parried with such excuses as the following:

1st. The presence of colored men in Faculty positions would retard the work; they would be unable
to secure funds from the white patrons of such institutions.

2d. That benefactors would not be so liberal if

the distribution of the funds were left to the discretion of the beneficiaries.

3d.   The ambition, though laudable and legitimate, is premature.

4th.   The colored people do not contribute largely to endowments and should not expect to have any voice in the control.

5th.   The colored man has a lack of confidence in himself and his race.

The fallacy of the first and second objections was brought forcibly to our mind by a conversation with Rev. J. C. Price, D. D., the honored and successful President of Livingston University, Salisbury, N. C.

Said Mr. Price: " In speaking to a gentleman on whom I called for aid for our work, I remarked, ' I come to you at a disadvantage, being a black man,' the usual custom being for white men to make the plea for such a cause.   He interrupted me by saying, ' Not so ; I would give you ten dollars where I would give a white man one, for I believe the colored man to be more sincerely interested in himself and his race than a white man can be for him.' "

The success of Livingston College, Tuskegee Normal School, Ala., and Wilberforce University of the A. M. E. Church, successfully refute the two first-named objections.

This is from the *Atlanta Defiance :*   Not long since $7000 were given to the Normal School at Tuskegee, Alabama.   This institution is run by 17 colored officers and teachers and the donors are two whites of Boston, Mass.   A few years ago no such faith as this would have been entertained in the *executive ability* of the Negro.   Gradually, the Negro grows in ability and in confidence of the balance of mankind.

This is worthy of note, and if the confidence here mentioned is to be measured by dollars, then North Carolina is far ahead.   Livingston College at Salisbury, a school managed entirely by colored men, has received four or five times $7000 from similar sources.

SELF-EDUCATION OF THE NEGRO.

A Successful Alabama School.

I came to Tuskegee, a characteristic Southern village of about 3000 inhabitants, for the sake of seeing the most successful effort of the Negro at self-education in this country.   I speak here of one large school which has been under Negro control from its inception, at which everything is done neatly, thoroughly, and with intelligent despatch.   That school is the Tuskegee Normal Colored School.   Here you have a small Hampton, which was founded, and has always been manned by the colored race.

This *Baby* Hampton has come into existence mysteriously, and almost as suddenly as did Aladdin's Palace.—*Chicago Inter-Ocean.*

In answer to the third objection, the colored man silently points to like institutions among the whites, of like grade, with the same number of graduates and the same number of years of growth, with their array of recruits from their own ranks, and he obstinately holds, in the face of the facts brought out by this survey, either the institutions for colored people are educationally a failure, or caste prejudice bars the doors against their colored graduates.

The fourth objection—the poverty that prevents endowments—must also fade to less brightness in the face of the substantial aid secured for Fisk University through the Jubilee Singers, and to Lincoln University and Hampton Institute through the eloquent discussions on the Negro problem, delivered from time to time by their graduates.

The last objection, that the Negro has a lack of confidence in himself and race, may appear at first sight to have some foundation, as the teachings of Slavery went far to engender a distrust in the minds of the race concerning their own abilities; but this lack of confidence has been met by ministers, lawyers, and physicians of the race, and has given way to an earnest pride in their success, and the belief that the presence of a fair percentage of colored men in the responsible position of Professors in these institutions would have beneficial results, and constitute one of the strongest reasons the alumni have for desiring this new departure in the management of such institutions.

The recent series of articles "On the Negro," appearing in the N. Y. *Independent,* show conclusively that the Negro has confidence in himself and his race, and in their ultimate success. A gradually developed but wide-spread feeling of dissatisfaction concerning this state of affairs has been coming to the surface in the alumni meetings of the various institutions for the last five years. In the case of Lincoln, Howard, Hampton and Biddle, the discussions have become public, the feeling has run high, and in each case the *local press* and *best thinkers* of both races are on the side of the alumni.

In the late discussion at Howard University, Washington, D. C., upon the filling of a vacancy occurring in the faculty, in answer to the spirit of opposition shown, said Senator Hoar: "I think the interests of the colored race will be much promoted as its members take the place of honor, requiring capacity, in other pursuits outside of politics."

Rev. Dr. Francis Grimke, in reviewing the circumstances of that hour, exclaims: "It was a spectacle which I shall never forget; I saw Gen. Kirkpatrick, an ex-

Confederate General, an ex-slaveholder, a member of the Democratic party, pleading for the appointment of a black man as Professor of Greek, under the very shadow of the nation's capitol, while old Abolitionists were diligently seeking to propagate the damnable heresy that it was immodest and presumptuous for black men to aspire to such positions, and by their voice and vote showing that they were determined to discourage as far as possible such aspiration.   An ex-Confederate General, an ex-slaveholder, a member of the Democratic party, and yet the most pronounced advocate of Negro advancement, on the Trustee Board of a black institution, made up largely of Northern men and Republicans !   An ex-slaveholder, and yet, with the most advanced ideas, with the clearest conception of the true policy to be pursued in the management of such institutions."   The closing words of his address on that memorable occasion were these— turning to his white brethren, he said : " We must decrease in these institutions, but they must increase."

The last arraignment of this spirit of caste was at the alumni meeting of Lincoln University, held June, 1886.   The matter had been broached to the faculty and trustees repeatedly.   The name of a thoroughly competent member of the alumni was presented to the faculty for professor, to fill a certain vacancy.   The fullest endorsement accompanied the recommendation of the alumni, but the whole matter was treated with bitter contempt, not even receiving a reply. A member of the Board of Trustees, when approached on the subject, admitted that possibly in the far future colored men would occupy such positions at Lincoln, but for the present it was not the policy of the institution. "The faculty of Lincoln," said he, " are as one family, and the admission of a colored professor and his family would be objectionable." On one occasion a young man, a graduate of this institution, being requested to speak, at the commencement exercises, broached the subject, offering to give $700 towards the endowment of a certain chair if occupied by a colored man. The speech was resented by the faculty, and the speaker was given to understand that the trustees and not the alumni made the appointments, and that hereafter he would not be invited to speak.

This state of affairs was freely commented upon by the alumni, and has created an actual enmity between the opposing forces. The alumni have endeavored to find the actual sentiment of the local clergy, and the wealthy patrons and friends of education on the matter; the following interviews give a partial idea of the real state of feeling regarding the matter :—

BOSTON, June 21, 1886.

SIR :—Referring to your note of the 17th inst., upon the question of caste in colored institutions, I can

answer in three words.   I see no reason why a colored
man, whose talents, requirements, and conduct entitle
him to a position socially and intellectually in scientific
institutions, should not be received and in the same
way as if he were not colored.

Yours truly,   BENJ. F. BUTLER.

If the equity of the well-worn balancer, *cæteris
paribus* (all the other qualifications on a par), be admitted, expressed or understood, then colored men
and women should have a preference in every colored
institution.   We go further, in non-essentials a slightly
imperfect par should not amount to a perfect bar.

—*Editor St. Joseph's Advocate, Baltimore, Md.*

The following is the opinion of Geo. D. McCreary,
a resident of Philadelphia, who has given largely to
educational institutions :—

" My opinion is that the question of color should
not enter into the management of the Lincoln or other
educational institutions for colored students, and if
fully qualified for the positions, no objection should be
made to their becoming members of the faculties or
trustees after graduation.   The opposition to such a
policy is indicative, either that the work of the institution is not thorough and the graduates only super-
ficially educated, or is based on the low plane of objection on account of color, with perhaps the desire on

the part of the incumbents to keep the places for themselves by preventing competition."

The following is an editorial comment from the Philadelphia *Press*, of June, 1886:—

CASTE IN THE COLORED COLLEGES.

It is difficult to see how the trustees of at least two of the colored colleges can escape "both horns" of the dilemma presented to them by Dr. N. F. Mossell at a meeting Wednesday evening of the alumni of Lincoln University. The university has been some thirty years in existence, and counts some 400 graduates; but none of these is represented in the faculty, and, as Dr. Mossell says, this circumstance indicates one of two things, "either that the education of the university is a failure, or that the caste prejudice forces the alumni out of these positions." Their exclusion is, at all events, anomalous. In other educational institutions it is the common practice to appoint graduates to faculty positions, whenever this may be done without detriment to the interests concerned, and there is no reason why the question should not obtain in a college for colored men as well as in one for white men.

Such, however, is the fact, and the alumni of colored colleges naturally feel very sore about it. As alumni, and particularly alumni belonging to a race which, but a generation ago, it was in some portions of this country a crime to instruct in the simplest rudiments of education, they are supposed to take an especial pride and an honorable interest in their colleges. They share, indeed, the interest which of late years has been especially evinced by alumni of all the colleges of the country.

The graduates of Howard, Biddle,* and Lincoln Universities have made urgent and repeated requests for representation in the faculties of those institutions. In the first named they have been measurably successful, we believe, but in neither of the others has their request met with the consideration they bespeak for it and they are convinced that the reason is that assigned by Dr. Mossell.

And if this is possible it ought to be done. For nothing can be less in accord with the principles on which the colored colleges were founded, than the fostering in the faintest degree, or the most impalpable form, of the spirit of caste, which these alumni charge upon their trustees, and which bears upon them far more cruelly than does ignorance, since it militates against their consideration as men.

" It gives me pleasure," said Rev. J. Wheaton Smith, the noted Baptist divine, "to say that complexion, whether light or dark, is not the test of manhood, and

---

* Biddle has at this date an entire colored faculty, who are doing good work,

should constitute no hindrance to either a pupil or teacher. In an institution of learning for the education of the colored race, other things being equal, I should give the preference to the darker hue. It is demanded by a ripening future, and the past crowded with un-numbered wrongs.

THE QUESTION OF COLOR SHOULD BE BARRED.

Said Rev. D. Baker, D. D., Pastor of the First Presbyterian Church, Washington Square, Philadelphia:

"I am of the decided opinion that the question of color should not enter in the least into the choice of professors or trustees in educational institutions; if a colored man is qualified, it is not unlikely that he might be on this account especially useful as an educator of his own race."

Rev. W. P. Breed, D. D., Pastor of West Spruce Street Presbyterian Church, Philadelphia, said:—

"On general principles the alumni of colored institutions should most undoubtedly be treated precisely as the alumni of all other institutions. The colored people are doing nobly, and they have my earnest wishes for their success and advancement."

Said Samuel Allen, of Philadelphia:—

"The Institute for Colored Youth, founded forty years ago, has been constantly under the care of the Society of Friends, by whom it was established. Having been connected with the Institute for Colored Youth as a manager of it, and somewhat familiar with it for quite a number of years, I am persuaded that the plan pursued there is an efficient one—of employing colored teachers in it, who have in almost every case proved themselves equal to the requirements. The instruction includes the higher branches of the knowledge of history, of mathematics and of the sciences ; all of which they teach to the entire satisfaction of the managers, and, as far as I know, to all concerned."

The sentiment of the advanced and liberal thinkers of the colored race given on the subject is as follows:—

Robert Purvis, of Philadelphia, says : " We demand that the same rule be applied to us as is applied to others. We ask no favors. We believe in the doctrine of equal rights. We ask no more, we will submit to no less; and in this especial instance I believe that, where the same qualifications as to character and fitness exists, the preference should be given to colored men as long as Colored Institutions exist. A fair show should be given in all other institutions. I am in favor of our being one people and American citizens."

WHAT FRED DOUGLASS THINKS OF THE SUBJECT.

" I have long noticed the tendency in colored institutions, as well as others, to repress and discourage the colored man's ambition to be something more than

a subordinate, when he is qualified to occupy superior
positions. It is a part of the old spirit of caste, a
legacy left us by slavery, against which we have to
contend. It is all the more difficult to meet because
in colored institutions under white control, it usually
assumes the guise of religion and a pious regard for
the happiness of the object of its disparagement, These
people play ' Miss 'Phelia to Topsy.' They would
have us among the angels in Heaven, but do not want
to touch elbows with us on earth."

WHAT DR. N. F. MOSSELL, OF PHILADELPHIA, SAYS.

" The best policy is not being pursued, when colored
men, qualified both by nature and acquirements, are
designedly excluded from the Faculties and Trustee
Boards of our colleges of learning. I think no reason-
able man will deny that."

OTHER OPINIONS.

Rev. Dr. B. F. Lee, editor of the *Christian Recorder*,
the organ of the A. M. E. Church, who was for a
number of years President of the Wilberforce University, said: " I think that there is a spirit of un-
rest among colored people in that they are losing
confidence in the management of these institutions.
They feel that they have been overlooked; that white
men are many times put over them as teachers when

persons of their own race could fill the position equally as well or better. The teachings of religion will never allow any one race to be its own absolute and exclusive educator, much less the educator of all races."

Prof. E. A. Bouchett, a graduate of Yale College, who is professor in the Institute for Colored Youth in Philadelphia, said: " The day has long gone by when an educated colored man was looked upon in this country as a curiosity. All persons of intelligence agree that the Negro is capable of undergoing the most severe mental training with credit to himself and his *alma mater*. The success of the graduates of colored colleges as teachers is abundantly attested, especially in the South and West; so the exclusion from the professor's chair in his own *alma mater* cannot be defended by alleging lack of ability or deficient capacity."

PROF. S. M. COLES, OF TEXAS,

who ten years ago took a second degree at Yale College, says : " Many of my college and class-mates are now occupying the best pulpits in the land ; many are tutors, professors, and principals of our best institutions for the education of youth. Now, it is claimed by our colored institutions that twenty years is not sufficient for them to develop fifty or seventy-five first-class scholarly men, from among seven million people, to occupy in equal ratios the honorable position for elevating their own race; if this be true, it must follow that there is a defect somewhere in the educational system; perhaps the present corps of instructors in these institutions are incompetent to fill the positions they occupy, or, perhaps, many are acting the role of Government officials, having a pleasant time at the people's expense.

"This is the conclusion we are driven to from their own statement.

"Yale, Harvard, Princeton, Amherst, and other white colleges, can in ten years accomplish more than those colored institutions in twenty.   Something is radically wrong!   But is it true that colored men have not been developed since the war sufficiently able to direct the work of educating their own race?   In the present condition of things this is unthinkable.

"Grover Cleveland, the President of the United States, wishes a suitable representative of the Government at the Court of Port Au Prince, and finds the abilities of a young colored man less than twenty-six years old, and less than three years from one of our American colleges, sufficiently matured to fill the position; and, again, desiring to fill another important position, the Liberian Minister, he calls upon an ex-slave, a gradu-ate from Lincoln University, in the class of 1873.

"My college-mate, our President, is a Democrat, yet
10

he does not ignore the Negro's ability.   In all departments of the Government colored men are placed in responsible positions, and they serve well—very few Belknaps and Moseses.   And equally true it is that colored institutions, conducted entirely by colored people, are just as efficient in their work as those conducted by the white for the colored students."

We demand educated colored teachers for all colored schools, because their *color identity* makes them more interested in the advancement of colored children than white teachers, and because colored pupils need the social contact of colored teachers.   Our people need social as well as educational advancement; and in this respect colored teachers can exercise potent influences, which would be lost if the selfish policy of employing white teachers obtain.—*Florida News.*

Large numbers of white people do not teach the Negro so much for the interest they have in him as they do for that they get.   In the second place there is always a tendency in a white teacher, however much he may be interested in the work, to crush out the manly and independent spirit that is essential to the full development of the mental powers.

They always keep prominent the fact that they think the Negro is their inferior, and try always to make him believe it.   In his attainments they virtually say to him, thus far shalt thou come and no farther.   If he is ambitious and will go beyond the mark they made for him, they have no more use for him.—*Missionary Worker.*

Nothing can be more detrimental to the future existence of these institutions than the belief and feeling among the alumni and patrons that such a state of affairs exists. The above opinions prove conclusively that the advanced feeling of the entire country is opposed to the fostering of such feeling under the guise of aid to the freedman. In an article by Charles T. Thiving, entitled "Colleges and their Graduates," in a late issue of the *Independent,* some forcible truths are stated which apply equally well to the matter under discussion. Says he :—

"The graduates of a college are at once its warmest friends and severest critics. The best friends of a college should naturally be found among its own graduates. Not only should a college foster the spirit of loyalty among its own graduates but these graduates may be and should be the most useful of its friends.

"In a large relation it may be added that alumni associations are of vast service. They tend to unify the best thought of some of the best men as to most important interests."

None of which can be the case if a feeling of repulsion and distrust has been aroused in the heart of the members of the alumni by a knowledge that the faculties and trustees are fostering caste prejudice against them. It is felt by the graduates that the caste prejudice is not shared by the patrons of these institutions who give freely and lovingly of their means, trusting to their trustees and faculties to attend to the distribution of it to the best advantage of those for whom it is contributed, but that caste is developed in the faculties, who are as a rule poor men and desire to secure and hold lucrative life positions for themselves and families. The purpose to ignore the Negro socially is another factor in the problem. They see that if a colored man becomes a member of the faculty he must be treated as other members of that department are treated; to this they will not submit; hence the colored man may not occupy the position. An odd feature of this caste prejudice is the strong hold it has upon the churches. The K. of L. and G. A. R. are open to him. The State institutions all over the country are fast becoming free to all, and where the schools are separate as Virginia State Normal, Mississippi State Normal, and Alabama State Normal Schools, the positions are given to competent colored teachers; but the church, the denominational schools under its control, the Christian Associations, cling to caste prejudice and sow the seed of distrust and unbelief in the heart of the black man.

VERSE.

By MRS. N. F. MOSSELL.

TWO QUESTIONS.

You ask me these two questions, dear:
What is the purest gift
That erst survived the fall?
And how that I should choose to die,
If I must die at all?

I'll answer thee: I know no purer gift than Love;
No greater bliss than just to dwell
Close held in Love's own clasp;
And glancing oft into the lovelight of thine eye;
Thus drifting from this earthly shore
See thee only, until I reached that land
Where love is love forever more.

LOVE'S PROMPTINGS.

Let thy life be precious unto thee, remembering this:
There is no joy that life doth hold for me,
But greater is that I may tell it thee;
No burden borne that bids me weep,
But would be greater far if thou didst lie
Quiet and still in thy last sleep.

I should be satisfied if I could lead thee to a
stronger walk,
That thy work should lie in some channel deep
and wide,

If heart and soul were attuned to some good
    purpose,
Though unto me through life, companionship
    should be denied,
Yet thus knowing, I should be satisfied.

LOVE'S FAILURE.

That love hath failed its task
That hath not moved to greater, purer deeds,
And I shall feel for evermore
That love hath failed to do all that I willed for
    thee,
Unless it moves to purer, loftier heights,
To nobler aims, that life may truly be
God's greatest, noblest gift, a heritage to thee.

RECOMPENSE.

Until life's end thy love shall be
The dearest boon earth holds for me,
And when death comes and leads us hence,
Then love shall find its recompense.

GOOD NIGHT.

Good night! Ah no, that cannot be
Good night that severs thee from me;
To dwell with thee in converse sweet,
And evermore thy presence greet,
Filling thy life with cheer and light,
Then each hour lost would bring good night.

To listen for thy footsteps' fall,
To answer when thy voice doth call,

To feel thy kisses warm and sweet,
Thy downward glance my lifted eye to greet,
To feel love's silence, and its might,
Then evermore 't would be good night.

To dwell with thee shut in, and all the world shut out,
Close clasped in love's own clasp,
And thus to feel that I to thee belong
And thou to me;
That nevermore on earth shall parting come,
But only at the bidding of that Loving One,
With will, power and hope to show love's might,
Then, and not till then, can come good night.

To know thy every helpful thought,
To look upon the universe and think God's thoughts
    after him,
To see the mystic beauty of music, poetry and art,
To minister unto thy every want,
To fill thy life with all the joy that woman's love can
    bring,
To shield thy life from evil, to bring thee good with
    love's insight,
This daily life would surely bring to each
The best good night.

LIFE.

A cry,
A sigh,
A sunny day,
An hour of play,
A budding youth,
A time of truth,

An "All is well,"
A marriage bell,
A childish voice,
That bids rejoice,
A fleeting hour
Of transient power,
A wounded heart,
Death's poisoned dart,
A fleeting tear,
A pall, a bier,
And following this,
Oh ! *loss* or *gain*,
An afterlife of *joy* or pain.

MY BABES THAT NEVER GROW OLD.

How oft in the gathering twilight
    I dream of the streets of gold,
Of my little angel children,
    " My babes that never grow old."

I can see my tiny woman
    With doll, and book held tight—
Keeping time with my every footstep,—
    From early morn until night.

And then, a white-robed figure
    Is kneeling at eventide,
And a voice lisps, "God bless papa,
    And dear little brother beside."

I see my laughing treasure,
  My darling baby boy,
With his little soft hands waving,
  And his cheeks aglow with joy.

The clap, clap, clap, for papa to come,
  To bring the baby a fife and drum,
Then each little pig that to market went,
  And the one wee pig at home.

In the bureau drawer hid out of sight
  Is the rattle, and cup, and ball;
The beautiful scrap-book laid away
  With dresses, and shoes and all;

And then, as the tears begin to flow,
  And grief to find a voice,
A soft cooing sound I hear at my side,
  That bids me ever rejoice.

I clasp her quick in a loving embrace
  My one lamb out of the fold,
Yet I ponder oft as I softly kiss,
  Will baby ever grow old?

Then cometh this thought to ease the pain,
  How God in his Book hath given,
" Suffer little children to come unto Me,
  For of such is the kingdom of heaven."

EARTH'S SORROWS.

There are nettles everywhere;
But smooth green grasses are more common still:
The blue of heaven is larger than the cloud.
—Mrs. Browning.

In the bright and pleasant spring-time
    We laid a dear form to rest :
The silvered head and the face of care,
    The hands close crossed on the breast.

We gave God thanks for the suffering done,
    The peace, and the joy and bliss,
That life had been lived, its trial were o'er,
    The next world's rest for the toil of this.

Then with the coming of winter's chill blast,
    Low down in its earthy bed
The child of our love we softly laid
    In its place with the lowly dead.

Friends crowded around with their whispers of love,
    But we thought of the vacant cot,
The sweet voice now for evermore stilled,
    And with sorrow we mourned our lot.

Then, with the silent fall of the leaves,
    The last bird left our nest,
Our arms were empty, the house was stilled,
    For our boy had gone to his rest.

We tried to repeat all words of prayer,
    All submissive and quiet thoughts ;

We tried to say God doth give and doth take,
   Blessed be the name of the Lord.

Earth's joys are many, its sorrows are few,
   And when in our arms was laid
A new little lamb to be trained for his fold,
   We said that our God was good.

With thankful hearts we took up once more
   The warp and the woof of life,
And out from our mind, our heart and thought,
   We thrust the struggle and strife.

And trusting God in His mercy still,
   The Man of sorrow and acquaint with grief,
We say this life to an end must come,
   Both its joys and sorrows be brief.

QUERY AND ANSWER.

You say that your life is shadowed
   With grief and sorrow and pain,
That you never can borrow a happy to-morrow
   And the future holds little of gain.

That a woman's life is but folly
   Scarce aught she may cheerfully do;
You think of your fate not with love but with hate,
   And wish that your days may be few.

You long with a bitter longing
   To enter the battle of life,

To strike some sure blow as onward you go
   To soften its warfare and strife.

You hate to be idly waiting
   As the years are drifting by,
A chance to be doing while duty pursuing
   And the years so swiftly fly.

Nay, a woman's life is the noblest
   That ever Old Time looked on,
Her lot both the rarest and fairest
   That ever the sun shone on.

Both dearer and sweeter and fairer
   Than any in all of this earth,
So full of its din of sorrow and sin
   Scarce feel we its cheer or its mirth.

Think oft of the hearts you may gladden,
   The tears you may soon chase away,
The many kind deeds that the wanderer needs
   To keep him from going astray.

Think oft of the mite of the widow,
   The cup of cold water given,
The love and faith mild of the little child
   That gaineth a seat in heaven.

Have you thought of the sweet box of ointment
   That Mary the Magdalene shed,
In its fragrance and beauty for love and not duty,
   Then wiped with the hair of her head?

Have you thought of the smile and the hand-clasp
　That met you some weary day,
That warmed you and fed you and hopefully led you
　To a safe and surer way?

Dear friend, when you faint by the wayside
　Oh think of these little things,
Then comfort the weary, the sad and the dreary
　And time will pass swift on its wings.

Let hope comfort, encourage and cheer you
　And help you to bravely say,
Not idly repining, but working and striving,
　Not hiding my talent away.

Then think not your lot has been hampered
　Or shadowed by grief or pain,
But up and adoing, still duty pursuing,
　The crown you surely must gain.

WORDS.

"Words fitly spoken are like apples of gold in pictures of silver."

"A word is a picture of a thought."

Words—idle words—ye may not speak,
　Without a care or thought;
For all that pass your lips each day
　With good or ill are fraught.

The words of joy, and peace, and love,
    You spoke at early morn,
Though time has passed and day is o'er,
    Are on their mission borne.

The threat of pain, and fear, and hate,
    You shouted in your wrath,
With all its deadly doing, still
    Is lying in your path.

Nay, e'en the tiny waves of air
    Your secret will not keep,
And all you speak when wide awake
    Is whispered, though you sleep.

A word may be a curse, a stab,
    And, when the sun is west,
Its onward course it still may run
    And rankle in some breast.

But words, small words, and yet how great,
    Scarce do we heed their power;
Yet they may fill the heart with joy,
    And soften sorrow's hour.

True hearts, by words, are ofttimes knit;
    Bound with a mystic tie,
Each golden link a word may loose;
    Yea, cause true love itself to die.

Mother, friendship, home and love;
   Only words, but Oh, how sweet!
How they cause the pulse to quicken,
   Eye or ear, whene'er they greet.

"Peace on earth, good will to men,"
   Are the words the angels spake,
And long ages echo them;
   Still their tones glad music make.

Each day we live, each day we speak;
   And ever an angel's pen
Doth write upon those pages fair
   The words of sinful men.

But one small word, but it must be
   A power for good or ill,
And when the speaker lieth cold
   May work the Master's will.

Then learn their power and use them well,
   That memory ne'er may bring
In time of mirth or lonely hour
   A sad or bitter sting.

Let only words of truth and love
   The golden silence break,
That God may read on record bright,
   She spoke for "Jesus' sake."

TELL THE NORTH THAT WE ARE RISING.

At the laying of the corner-stone of Atlanta University in 1879 occurred the incident recorded in the following lines.

There was the human chattel
Its manhood taking ;
There in each dark brain statue,
A soul was waking.
The man of many battles,
The tears his eyelids pressing,
Stretched over those dusky foreheads
His one-armed blessing.

And he said : " Who hears can never
Fear for nor doubt you ;
What shall I tell the children
Up North about you ? "
Then ran round a whisper, a murmur,
Some answer devising;
And a little boy * stood up—" Massa,
Tell 'em we're rising." †

Tell the North that we are rising;
Tell this truth throughout the land—
Tell the North that we are rising—
Rising at our God's command.

---

* R. R. Wright, the little hero of this poem, has now grown to manhood and occupies the responsible position of President of the Georgia State Industrial College for Colored Youth.

† Whittier.

Could the bravest say it better?
Was the child a prophet sent?
From the mouths of babes and sucklings
Are the words of wisdom lent.

Tell the North that we are rising;
East and West the tidings go;
Tell this truth throughout the nation—
Tell it to both friend and foe.

Tell our true and tried friend Lincoln,
Tell our Grant and Sumner true—
Tell them each that we are rising,
Knowing we have work to do.

See the child before us standing,
All his heart and life aglow,
Backward flit the years of sorrow;
Onward hopes, bright visions flow.

All his life has lost its shadow,
Filled is it with coming light;
Hope and Faith again triumphant
Make the present glad and bright.

Thus the keynote of our future
Touched he with his childish hand;
In his words the inspiration
Lingering yet throughout the land.

And the brave old poet Whittier
Treasured up his song in verse,

11

That the myriads yet to follow,
Might anon the tale rehearse.

Those who then wore childhood's garland
Now are true and stalwart men ;
Those who bore war's dreadful burdens,
Friend and foe have died since then.

But we still would send the message
To our friends where'er they roam,
We are rising, yea, have risen:
Future blessings yet will come.

Noble son of noble mother,
When our hearts would shrink and falter,
We yet treasure up your message,
Laying it on freedom's altar.

We with courage strive to conquer,
'Till as England's Hebrews stand
We are neither slaves nor tyrants,
But are freemen on free land.

THE MARTYRS OF TO-DAY.

By the swiftly flowing rivers,
    In the fertile Southern land,
Gathered there from lane and highway,
    Scores of men, an earnest band.

Not with brows of snowy whiteness,
    Not with chiseled features rare ;

Rather cheeks of sable darkness,
　　Yet was God's own image there.

Do they fear the chain of bondage?
　　Do they fear the lash or mart?
Slaves ignoble! do they tremble—
　　Sadly lack the freeman's heart?

　　·　　　·　　　·　　　·　　　·

See, one in their midst—a brother—
　　Reads of blood and deeds of pain—
Deeds of cruelty and outrage—
　　That with horror chill each vein.

He, with solemn tone and gesture,
　　Furrowed brow and wearied hand,
Reads this tale so weird and solemn,
　　To this earnest, thinking band.

　　·　　　·　　　·　　　·　　　·

In the silence of the midnight,
　　Decked in robes of dingy white,
On their foamed and maddened chargers,
　　And with features hid from sight,

Ride a band of fearless South'rons,
　　With a ruthless iron will;
Ride their foamed and maddened chargers,
　　Through the vale and o'er the hill.

And they give to none the quarter
　　Which the brave are wont to give;
Man nor woman, babe nor suckling,
　　Be they black, are 'lowed to live.

These now all were made to perish
　　By the flower of Southern life;
And the deed is yet commended
　　By both Southern maid and wife.

　　.　　　.　　　.　　　.　　　.　　　.

Long, too long, our race has suffered,
　　Both from church and school and state;
Trade and ballot long denied us,
　　Yet our friends still council, wait.

Must we, then, give up the struggle?
　　Must we sail for Afric's shore?
Must we leave this land we've toiled in?
　　Must it swim again with gore?

Must we wait with greater patience?
　　Must we say, "Oh, Lord, forgive?
Must we love these worse than foemen,
　　Who forbid us die or live?

We must ponder Calvary's lesson;
　　View our martyred Saviour's fate;
Work and pray, with faith in heaven;
　　Right must conquer—therefore wait.

A GREETING SONG TO OUR BROTHERS IN AFRICA.

We send you a greeting, our brothers,
　　Our brothers over the sea,
Who have sailed away to that sunny land,
　　Its light and blessing to be.

We have heard of your safe arrival,
　　Of the work you have chosen to do,
Of the little ones gathered together
　　To hear the truths old and yet new.

We ask for God's blessing upon you,
　　As we lift up our voices in prayer,
And by faith we know you receive it,
　　Though we worship not with you there.

The harvest is great, let reapers be many;
　　May ye sow and bountifully reap;
May your lives be long and useful,
　　And mourned your eternal sleep.

CHILD OF THE SOUTHLAND.

　　Child of the Southland
　　Baring thy bosom,
　　Feeling hate's poisoned dart,
　　Reeking with venom,
　　God looks upon you,
　　Seeth your sorrow;
　　Great the awakening,
　　Dawneth the morrow,
　　Lifteth the burden,
　　Greed placed upon you.
　　Mercy is watching
　　Justice but sleeping,
　　Angels above you,
　　Their vigils keeping;

Cometh the future,
With its hope laden,
Keepeth the promise,
Made us in Eden;
Ethiop stretcheth
Forward her hand,
Graspeth the staff of life,
Gaineth the promised land.

WHY BABY WAS NAMED CHRIS.

I told mamma I was tired of noise,
Tired of marbles, and tops and toys,
I had nobody to play with me.
So I didn't enjoy myself, you see.

I told her I guessed that I would pray
To dear old Chris that very day,
And tell him then, somehow or other,
I wanted him to send me a baby brother.

I knelt right down by my little chair,
As quick as I could, and said my prayer,
I went to bed right soon that night
And jumped up quick with the Christmas light.

In my little bare feet I softly crept
Down to the room where my ma slept,
And there, by the mantel, fast asleep
Down in a cradle wide and deep,
Lay a dear little baby brother.

He had a round face and a little red nose,
Ten little fingers, and ten little toes,
Two black eyes, and a dimpled chin,
That's where the angels had kissed him.

So we named him " Chris," only that,
And he grows so big, and rosy, and fat,
He rolls and tumbles about when we play,
But never gets hurt, for I always say
I'll be right good, so if Chris goes by,
He'll surely see that I always try
To 'preciate my Christmas present.

ONLY.

Only a baby, but strong and bright,
Making us happy from morn until night,
And knitting together with cords of love,
Those who were joined by the God above.

Only a boy, with his frolic and fun,
His marbles, and tops, and miniature gun,
But time rolls by, and leaves in his stead
The man, tender of heart, and wise of head.

Only a girl, with her dolls and play,
Her loving glance, and dainty way—
But the summers have fled with a sweet surprise,
And a stately maiden gladdens our eyes.

The maiden, now, is the matron dear,
That with tender counsel doth little ones rear;
And we vow in our hearts, our lips shall ne'er curl
As we scornfully say, " Only a girl!"

Only a flower in a mossy bed;
By sun, and by rain, it was gently fed,
And now in the room of a suffering one,
Its mission fulfilled, its work is done.

Only a word, but it chanced to fall
On the ear of one forsaken of all,
And a heart, bowed down in its bitterness,
Arose once more its God to bless.

Only a song, a gladsome lay,
Sung cheerily on through a weary day;
'Twas a simple tune in a merry strain,
But it eased a heart of its burden of pain.

Only a thought, full of wondrous power,
Born in the need of a stricken hour,
Yet it grew and thrived, and taking root
In the hearts of many, it bore much fruit.

Only a prayer, from a heart, sad and lone,
It passed on its way to the Great White Throne;
'Twas spoken in faith, 'twas answered in love,
And a sinner turned to his God above.

BEAUTIFUL THINGS.

Beautiful eyes are those that see
God's own children that should be;
Beautiful ears are those that hear
Their little footsteps lingering near.

Beautiful lips are those that press
Stained ones with fond caress;
Beautiful hands are those that grasp
The blind and erring with gentle clasp.

Beautiful feet are those that lead
Wandering ones the path to heed;
Beautiful hearts are those that beat
In sympathy warm at the mercy-seat.

Beautiful faces are those we see
And bless our God for memory;
Beautiful forms are those that move
Joyfully forward, on missions of love.

Beautiful homes are those that teach
Patient acts and kindly speech;
Beautiful lives are those that give
Others the strength and courage to live.

Beautiful words are those we spake,
Timid and tearful, "For Jesus' sake;"
Beautiful thoughts are those that fly
On wings of love to God on high.

Beautiful prayers are those we raise
For them that turn from wisdom's ways;
Beautiful songs are those we sing
When sinners own our Lord and King.

Beautiful wills on God's work bent,
Beautiful errands of good intent;

Beautiful heaven smiling above,
Beautiful truth that " God is love."

Beautiful promise in God's own Book—
Free to all who will only look;
Beautiful crown when cross we bear;
Beautiful ransomed ones, bright and fair.

Beautiful Saviour, the Crucified Lamb,
All wise, all loving, the Great I Am;
Beautiful Sabbath of perfect rest—
Beautiful day that God has blest.

Beautiful sleep, all joy and gain,
No grief or loss, neither sorrow or pain;
Beautiful rest with work well done;
Beautiful saints around God's throne.

THREE HOURS.

"Work while it is day; the night cometh when no man can work."

" Do noble things, not dream them all day long, and so make life, death and that vast forever one grand, sweet song."

MORNING.

A mother sat in the rosy dawn
    Of a morning bright and fair,
Her arms are round her firstborn son,
    Her breath is in his hair.

My little son to my God I will give
    Ere yet his tongue can lisp;
And all the days my boy shall live
    Shall be spent in His service rich.

But the years pass on and he grows apace,
 His limbs are round and free,
His feet can tread the meadow path,
 His eyes its wonders see.

But the mother is busied with household care,
 And ever, like Martha of old,
Her heart is troubled with many things,
 And the Saviour's love untold.

The little child is bountifully fed,
 His form is daintily robed,
And mind and heart are stored with good—
 Only the soul is starved.

NOON.

'Tis noon of day and noon of life,
 And the infant is now a youth,
And the mother's heart to its depth is stirred,
 As it feels the bitter truth.

That years have passed with their length of days,
 And the babe no longer a child,
Though loved by all, by many praised,
 Is not loving the Master's precepts mild.

So carefully striving day by day
 Lost footsteps to retrace,
The mother's heart goes blindly on,
 Prays for the seed a resting-place.

But the youth is filled with the hour's conceit;
  The ground is stony and choked with weeds,
And seeds of evil already sown
  Must be rooted out ere we sow good seeds.

And now again the household care
  Is ruling heart and mind,
And neighbors oft her bounty share,
  And love the eye doth blind.

NIGHT.

And now again 'tis set of sun,
  And close of life's fair day;
The youth has passed to manhood's hour,
  But only *lips* can pray.

No longer may the mother voice,
  In accents sweet and mild,
With holy words of Bible lore,
  Still guide her little child.

In college walls by scoffers thronged,
  No precious word made household truth,
Is brought to him, by memory fair,
  To guide his erring youth.

His life no longer the mother may shape,
  Forever lost is the precious hour;
Now only God can the wrong undo,
  By the help of His mighty power.

O, mothers dear! throughout our land,
  Its acres fair and wide!

With little ones your daily care,
  Now walking by your side,

Keep ever this truth before you;
  At morn, at night, alway,
That to teach the love of the Saviour,
  His precepts to obey,

With kindly lips and true,
Is a work that lies ever before you,
The best that you can do.

Let not the hours pass idly on,
  'Till morn and noon and night have come,
And all your work lay idly by,
  And remain perhaps forever undone ·

But gird your heart up to the work;
  Let every day some Bible truth
Be sown in the heart and mind of each child,
  To guide him on in his tender youth.

And when the close of life shall come
  And all your work shall cease,
The Soul to its Giver shall return
  To a life of endless peace.

THE STORY OF A LIFE.

CHILDHOOD—HOME.

A precious gift our God has given
  To bless declining years,
Anew we feel our sins forgiven,
  And eyes o'erflow in grateful tears.

A little child with gentle ways,
   The darling household pet,
Swiftly passing, peaceful days,
   The jewel is ours yet.

The child has passed to bloom of youth
   A maiden fair of face,
With heart of love and lips of truth,
   Doth still our fireside grace.

The skilful hands and winsome ways
   Win love without a thought;
And words of cheer and songs of praise
   Are given, though all unsought.

A time of sadness follows now,
   And then a Saviour's love;
A grateful band we humbly bow,
   And thank our Friend above.

But grown to years of maidenhood
   The heart is not our own;
Though home is dear and God is love,
   The sweet content has flown.

MAIDENHOOD—LOVE.

A quiet room, an easy chair,
   With firelight all aglow,
Two loving hearts beat happily—
   Ah, quickly time doth flow.

A breathless parting for a year,
   A tear from sweet, dark eye,
A joyful meeting at its close·
   Ah, quickly time doth fly.

A fancied bond of friendship,
   A whispered confidence,
A wicked heart to prompt deceit,
   And happiness flies hence.

A stolen page, a recreant love,
   Ah, what is left to tell!
A broken heart, a weeping throng,
   And then—a funeral knell.

A wounded heart, a home bereft,
   No daughter grace now lends,
Long, weary years of loneliness,
   And thus the story ends.

WOMANHOOD—DEATH.

But to our hearts with healing balm
   This thought brings memory fair,
The weary couch had long become
   "A Christ-held hammock of prayer,"

Which faithful friends, a loving band,
   Had twisted with promises bright,
And angels fair with loving hands
   Had gathered and fastened tight.

Her words of love are with us still:
  " So quiet I lie 'neath the eternal sky,
" Biding the time when God, in His will,
  " Shall take me to dwell with Him on high."

Though the beautiful form is laid away
  And our home is no more blest,
Though joy had its hour and sorrow its day,
  We know that with Jesus is rest.

Princeton, N. J.

APPENDIX.

Too Late to be Classified.

Miss Sarah E. Tanner has been appointed Principal and instructor in English Literature and Industrial Drawing at the Colored Normal and Industrial School, Bordentown, N. J.

Mrs. Mary H. Valodus, a native of Pennsylvania, trained in the Presbyterian Church, later active in missionary work in the A. U. M. E., was licensed to preach by Bishop Williams and has erected within the space of six years two churches, one at Rome, the other at Amsterdam, N. Y. Mrs. Valodus is now endeavoring to establish an Agricultural and Industrial School in Central, N. Y.

Miss Ellen Nowell Ford, of Oakland, Cal., now of New York, has received a diploma certifying to the excellence of crayon work exhibited by her in the New York State exhibit at the World's Fair, Chicago, 1893.

Mrs. M. A. McCurdy, of Rome, Ga., is editor of the *Woman's World.*

Miss Fisher, of New Bedford, by obtaining a certain number of subscribers to the *Woman's Era*, has been placed in the Boston Training School of Music.

Miss Frances A. Davis and Mrs. Fanny Ridgel are laboring as missionaries in West Africa.

A number of young women have graduated as trained nurses from the Provident Hospital, Chicago, and it is also said that Johns Hopkins has twenty-four Afro-American women graduates.

Miss Lucy Thurman is National Superintendent of Temperance Work among the Afro-Americans. Mrs. F. E. W. Harper is National Organizer of the same work. Amanda Smith is World's Evangelist of the W. C. T. U.